A COMM

LET'S TALK ABOUT
The Book of
EPHESIANS

DR. MELVIN H. KING

ZYIA CONSULTING
Illuminate & Transcend

ZYIA CONSULTING
Illuminate & Transcend

Zyia Consulting
Book Writing & Publishing Company
www.nyishaddavis.com
nyisha.d.davis@gmail.com
313.346.6189

Unless otherwise noted, all Scripture quotations are taken from www.biblestudytools.com;
GOD's Word translation (GW) or King James Version.

Cover Design: Zyia Consulting, LLC

Cove Image Credit: ArtCoreStudios - Retrieved from https://pixabay.com/users/artcorestudios-704771/

ISBN: 978-0-578-99663-9

Printed in the United States of America.

Dr. Melvin H. King

Pastor Melvin H. King knows the power of influence and understands the importance of walking out GOD's plan for his life by Faith. As a native of Atlanta, Georgia, born one of three children to Melvin & Christine King, integrity, persistence, and a love for GOD was instilled in him. He was taught the importance of having the ability to empower oneself by keeping GOD at the center of his life at all times. He is no stranger to hearing the voice of GOD. For at the young age of twelve, he began his journey when he received his calling into the ministry. Not quite understanding the fullness of that call, Pastor King knew, one day, that GOD the HOLY SPIRIT, would give him a clear and measurable vision of how GOD, the Father, desired to use him in the work of the ministry.

After graduating from C.L. Harper High School, Pastor King continued to further his education at Tuskegee University in Alabama, where he studied Architecture. While in attendance at Tuskegee University, he servedas Executive Committee Director of the Student Government Association (S.G.A.). Where he was responsible for all freshmen activities. He later continued his educational pursuits at Clayton State College, where he enrolled in the Architecturalprogram. In 1990, Pastor King entered into the International Brotherhood of Electrical Workers (I.B.E.W.) program; completing studies toward becoming an Electrician, and became a certified Electrician in 1996.

Although Pastor King was pursuing his education, he never forgot the day that GOD called him. By the age of twenty-one, GOD the HOLY SPIRIT gave him the understanding that he needed. Pastor King responded by accepting his calling into the ministry. Under the tutelage, guidance, and leadership of Bishop Dreyfus C. Smith, Pastor of Wings of Faith Ministries in Atlanta, Georgia, Pastor King walked into the beginning of his life as a minister of JESUS CHRIST, our Savior. He later received his license to minister the Gospel on December 10, 1989,and was later ordained in October 1994.

In August 1991, as Pastor King continued his journey being led by the SPIRIT of GOD, he moved to Los Angeles, California, where he served in the ministry under the late Dr. J.W. Evans, his uncle. Pastor King then enrolled into La Verne University School of Theology. He later obtained a degree and a Baccalaureate Certificate in Christian Ministry, both from The King's University, founded by Pastor Jack Hayford. Pastor King completed post-graduate studies at Oxford University in Oxford, England in 2009.

On January 11, 1998, Pastor King was elected the Pastor of the Mary Magdalene Missionary Baptist Church in Los Angeles, California. He was installed on March 1, 1998. Under his leadership at Mary Magdalene, over 4,000 souls surrendered their lives to Christ. Two years later, on October 26, 2000, his accomplishments continued, and he became a member of the Macedonia International Fellowship under the leadership and guidance of Bishop Kenneth C. Ulmer, in Johannesburg, South Africa, in an association of pastors representing ministries in South Africa and the U.S.A.

While holding steadfast to the Word of GOD and the values that his parents taught him, Pastor King, remaining firm on his promise to GOD to not compromise His Word, stepped out by Faith and resigned as Pastor of Mary Magdalene. GOD honored his Faithfulness and on October 10, 2010, Divine Deliverance Ministries (10D/10D/10M) was birthed. The ministry at DDM continues to grow strong as it holds on to the mission of spreading the Gospel to the ends of the world, and inviting others to become new Disciples of JESUS CHRIST.

On April 18, 2015, Pastor King received his Doctorate of Divinity degree from Saint Thomas Christian University, and is acknowledged as a visionary, with the ability to preach and teach the Word of GOD with simplicity and accuracy. Pastor King is noted for his upbeat, enthusiastic style as he continues to dynamically lead others into the "Next Dimension" of their journey in CHRIST, just as he has. He remains committed to restoring the Kingdom of GOD, preaching the Gospel and lifting up the name of JESUS!

Pastor King additional career highlights:

- Featured three times on the television talk show "Oh Drama."
- Appeared on the television show "Raising Whitley" broadcasted by the Oprah Winfrey Network (OWN).
- Produced a nationally televised ministry on the BET Network.
- 2004 received a Certificate of Recognition of Completion from The Los Angeles Division of the FBI Citizens' Academy.
- 2014 received The Senior Pastor Institute Certificate of Completion from Dr. R.A. Vernon.

Table of Contents

Introduction to the Book of Ephesians

So, before we go into the book of Ephesians, let's discuss what we already know about the book of the Galatians. The Book of Galatians was a letter written to the Christian believers in a city called Galatia. As a matter of fact, Paul's message was to several churches in the city of Galatia. Paul's message to the believers was a message of freedom and liberty. He taught that everything CHRIST endured on the cross freed and delivered us from bondage. We no longer have to be in bondage because through CHRIST we have freedom.

As citizens of Galatia were converted into the freedom of CHRIST, they dealt with bondage religiously and politically. Paul's message to the Galatians believers was that even though you are experiencing oppression both religiously and politically, there's freedom in CHRIST. There's liberty in JESUS.

The Jews had a problem with Paul's message, because they were trying to keep the Christians in bondage by making them follow the Mosaic Law. They thought to get to heaven or get GOD's approval into heaven, you had to also practice the law. Paul's teachings taught them that their works did not give them access into heaven, but what they believed did; the work CHRIST did on the cross is enough for us to receive salvation.

When anything else is added as a requirement to the work JESUS has already done on the cross, it then becomes an insult to the sacrifice JESUS made on the cross. If we say it takes what JESUS did on the cross and something else, it is to say that what JESUS did on the cross was not enough. I don't know about you, but what took place on the cross was good enough for me.

A lot of churches spend more time practicing and following their traditions than they do worshipping GOD. And GOD is not moved by our traditions; HE's moved by our Faith. That's why Hebrews 11:6 says, And without Faith, it is impossible to please GOD. Not by our works; but by our Faith. Paul was trying to get the Galatians to understand that they did not need to practice the Mosaic law to please GOD, they just needed Faith. Trusting GOD by Faith is a lot easier than trying to please HIM by works. GOD wants us to trust HIM by our Faith and not trust HIM according to some law.

The message Paul taught the Galatians freed them from the law. Anytime GOD frees you from any type of bondage, it allows you to worship HIM in SPIRIT. Bondage hinders you from worshiping GOD in SPIRIT because you can't worship GOD in SPIRIT if you are in bondage. Why? Because the Gospel can't be a message of liberty and freedom if we turn it into a gospel of restrictions and obligations. We know GOD doesn't do bondage!

Because remember what the Bible says, GOD is a SPIRIT: and they that worship him must worship him in spirit and in truth. Not by being in bondage to restrictions and obligations. (John 4:24 KJV) The Mosaic law was/is filled with restrictions and obligations. You can't worship GOD in SPIRIT, if the truth is, you are obligated by restrictions. That's why Paul's message to the Galatians was a message of freedom and liberty. For those of you that have studied the book of Galatians, you are to break out into hives when anything tries to restrict you and obligate you; because that's bondage! When you think about it, every single religion known to mankind is a religion of works; except the Gospel of JESUS CHRIST.

Every religion gives you a list of stuff you must do for GOD to be pleased and accept you. But the Gospel's message is that salvation is a gift; that JESUS CHRIST has done all the work for you. So, either you accept the free gift of salvation, or you reject the free gift of salvation. But, you definitely don't need to work for it. Who in their right mind would reject the

8

free gift of salvation? Someone who doesn't have Faith. The Jews in Galatia were trying to convince the Christans in Galatia that along with the work JESUS did on the cross, they also needed the laws of traditions.

Paul taught that once we become saved, we now have control over our flesh because we are no longer in bondage to our flesh. Once the HOLY SPIRIT realizes that you are no longer in bondage, your Temple then becomes HIS dwelling place. The HOLY SPIRIT will only dwell where there is freedom and liberty. Why? Who the Son sets free is truly free indeed. (John 8:36) Now how many of you know that you are free?

As we enter into the book of Ephesians, it will probably surprise you that this letter probably shouldn't be called Ephesians. The reason I say that is because we don't know to whom this letter was written. But the Christians in Ephesus were certainly among those to whom this letter was directed. In other words, there were others. So, it would be safe to say this letter was written to several communities that surrounded Ephesus.

Now, I must give you all this because this is going to be very important. The first four letters to The Churches, which are Romans, 1st and 2nd Corinthians' and Galatians' primary message was CHRIST in you. Meaning, what CHRIST is intended to accomplish in us. But when we get to the book of Ephesians, the theme changes from CHRIST In You to You In CHRIST. And that's Ephesians through the book of Philemon. The message in these letters is going to teach us how to discover what it means for us to be in CHRIST.

In the book of Ephesians through Philemon, we're going to be dealing with 'You In CHRIST.' One of the most famous and most quoted Scriptures is found in the book of Ephesians. It tells us that we wrestle not against flesh and blood, but against principalities, against powers, against the rulers of the darkness of this world, against spiritual wickedness in high places. (Ephesians 6:12 KJV)

As a matter of fact, in Ephesians 3:10, we're going to learn that the headquarters of the powers of evil is also in the spirit realm. This is why it's important for you to be in CHRIST because you can have CHRIST in you. You can have all the gifts of the SPIRIT in you. But if you don't put those gifts to use, they become useless. Basically, when you are in CHRIST, you operate in a different realm as a believer. Paul's message to us now is, by us being in CHRIST, HE wants us to focus on us being The Church; not the building, but the believer! Some people tend to think of The Church as something we go to, we attend, or that is separate from us that we give our donations to.

But Paul, in the letter to the Ephesians, wants us to realize that we are The Church. And when you start thinking that GOD's church as the building or our denomination, it's easy to take the blame off of us and place it on the organization. So, instead of blaming you, you blame the ministry. When you can say, The Church is not doing this and The Church is not doing that, well, if you're supposed to represent The Church, to say what The Church is not doing is admitting exactly what you're not doing yourself. "They're messy," what that really means is, 'you're messy.' Because you know your church better than anyone. "They're fake," Oh, Ok! Are they fake, or are you fake?

In our studies, regarding this letter to the Ephesians, we're going to see Paul trying to get the believers to see themselves as 'The Church,' which represents The Body of CHRIST. In his book, "Adventuring Through The Bible" by Ray Stedman, he says, one way Paul tries to get the believers to understand their role as The Church is by using six different metaphors. The first metaphor Paul uses is 'The Church' represents The Body; or should I say 'a Body.' Ephesians 1:22-23 says, And GOD placed all things under HIS feet and appointed him to be head over everything for The Church, which is HIS body, the fullness of him who fills everything in every way. Watch this. We are not the Head, but every believer represents a part of The Body. What is the purpose of The Body?

First thing, The Body is the expression of the Head. It's supposed to express and perform the desires of the Head. If my hand rubs my head, it's not because my hand had a desire to rub my head. My hands only did what the head told it to do. The only time The Body does not execute the commands of the Head is when it's involuntary.

For example, if I hit a certain part of my knee, it will automatically cause my leg to jump involuntarily; involuntary reflex. The head didn't tell my leg to move. Something hit it and caused it to move. Spiritually we can call that spiritual wickedness. That's why it's important to put on the whole armor of GOD, which we will also be talking about in Ephesians. Putting on the whole armor of GOD protects us from spiritual wickedness hitting our bodies that could cause The Body to act out involuntarily. The armor that GOD provides for us allows us to stand against the wiles of the devil. (Ephesians 6:11)

Have you ever noticed people in The Body of CHRIST that will lie and not even flinch? It's because they don't have on the whole armor of GOD. When spiritual wickedness hits them, it causes them to respond involuntarily. Anytime you can sin and not even flinch, it's because you're not getting the signal from the head, and something is causing you to respond involuntarily.

Then the second metaphor that Paul uses in the book of Ephesians is The Church is the Temple. Ephesians 2:21-22 says, In HIM the whole building is joined together and rises to become a holy temple in the LORD. And in HIM, you too are being built together to become a dwelling in which GOD lives by HIS SPIRIT. The purpose of us being The Temple is, so we can be effective for HIS purpose. When we are The Temple, we become HIS dwelling place where GOD can enter HIS Temple and be able to say, "I'M home." You never want to be the cause of GOD not finding peace in HIS own home.

When there is no peace in your home, it causes you not to want to go home. You don't want GOD to have to drive around the neighborhood because HE doesn't want to be at home. Why? Because GOD is not the author of confusion. (1 Corinthians 14:33) And whenever there's confusion in the Temple, GOD decides not to come home. When GOD dwells in the Temple, you want to make sure HE's comfortable being at home. So the question is, is GOD comfortable in your Temple or is HE driving around the neighborhood?

The third metaphor that Paul uses is that The Church is a mystery. Now, we'll deal more with that when we get to chapter 3 of Ephesians. Basically, when Paul calls The Church a mystery, it's up to every believer to make known the wisdom of GOD to spiritual wickedness. To educate spiritual wickedness to the wisdom of GOD, you definitely have to be in CHRIST.

The fourth metaphor that Paul uses is The Church is a new self. In other words, Therefore if any man be in CHRIST, he is a new creature: old things are passed away; behold, all things are become new. (2 Corinthians 5:17) The reason all things are new is because everything we lost from Adam has been regained in CHRIST.

The fifth metaphor is The Church is a bride. As believers, it's our job to make sure that we make HIS bride look virtuous and not look like a whore. If each one of us represents 'The Church,' as HIS bride, we should always make ourselves presentable. Think about it, what groom wants HIS bride to resemble a prostitute? GOD says, "I don't want our relationship status to be listed as 'Complicated,' I want everybody to know that you're MY lady. You're not a side-chick. You're MY bride. Furthermore, you're not an option; you're priority. A royal priesthood, a holy nation, someone who has been chosen. (1 Peter 2:9) In Ephesians 5, Paul is going to describe the true nature of The Church and that is, The Church is a bride. So, we should act like a bride and not act like a side-chick.

The last metaphor, which is metaphor six, Paul tells the Ephesians, The Church is a soldier. (Ephesian 6:10-18) So, we go from being a bride to being a soldier. And it's nothing like having a bride that knows how to fight and intercede amid spiritual warfare. The last thing you want is someone who is going to panic in times of trouble. When Paul says, The Church is a soldier, this is when Paul talks to us about putting on the whole armor of GOD. By putting on the whole armor of GOD, GOD has equipped HIS bride not to be scared to fight.

Paul talks to us about the importance of putting on the whole armor of GOD because when we put on the whole armor of GOD, it causes us to walk in the six different metaphors that Paul uses all at once. When we are equipped with the right armor:

- The right armor causes The Body to execute orders from the Head.
- The right armor makes sure there is peace in GOD's temple.
- The right armor will make known the mysteries of GOD to spiritual wickedness in high places. We will not wrestle in the flesh and will know what to say in the spirit.
- The right armor will cause us to appreciate our new selves.
- The right armor empowers us to be a righteous bride. It's amazing how Paul discusses the new self and then talks about being a bride. Even if you were a liar, fornicator, sinner, or former anything the right armor will cause you to walk in your new self which is GOD's bride.
- But last and definitely not least, the right armor will also help you
- stand like a soldier.

As 'The Church,' it is our six-fold calling that GOD has equipped us as believers. So, basically, every believer is a part of The Body. Every believer is GOD's temple. Every believer is supposed to make known the wisdom of GOD to spiritual wickedness, be a new self, and understand they are the Bride of CHRIST and a soldier.

In Ephesians chapter 4 verse 1, this is Paul's message to every believer, therefore, the prisoner of the Lord, beseech you that ye walk worthy of the vocation wherewith ye are called. (NKJV) The GOD's Word Translation says, I, a prisoner in the Lord, encourage you to live the kind of life which proves that GOD has called you.

Chapter 1

The Body

Greeting
Verses 1-3

Before we get into chapter 1, let's make sure we understand who Paul's audience is. It has been established in the introduction that Paul's target audience is the Christians in Ephesus. Anytime you study any book of the Bible, it is always good to know the audience the book was written to. This letter to the Ephesians was a little different from the other letters Paul had written to the earlier. In previous letters, Paul was dealt with certain situations and problems that were going on in that city.

So, when we enter into Ephesians Chapter 1, we see Paul starts off this letter by greeting his audience. For verse 1 says, From Paul, an apostle of CHRIST JESUS by GOD's will. To GOD's holy and Faithful people who are united with CHRIST in the city of Ephesus. Good will and peace from GOD our Father and the Lord JESUS CHRIST are yours! What did you notice about Paul's greeting to the Ephesians that was different from his other letters? In Paul's other letters to the believers, he is more personal. Instead of Paul starting his letter by saying greetings brothers and sisters, in this letter to the Ephesians, he's not as personal as he has been. Paul is more formal to his audience. The assignment that Paul had to the Ephesians was one of a messenger. It seems like Paul is actually introducing himself to his audience, instead of just going in and telling them about themselves, like he did in his letters to the Corinthians and to the Galatians.

After Paul greets his audience and introduces himself as an apostle of JESUS, watch what he says in verse 1, ...by GOD's will. The reason he makes this statement is that Paul is saying that he didn't call himself to be an apostle of CHRIST, it's ...by GOD's will that he is an apostle of JESUS CHRIST. In other words, Paul is very strategic in his approach to his audience, because his message is about everyone playing their part in The Body. Paul said, let me start off by letting you know my part in The Body. See, I'm not an arm trying to be the foot. My part in The Body is according to GOD's will. So, if The Body is not functioning properly, it's not because I'm not playing my part. My part is to be an apostle of JESUS CHRIST. So, let's figure out if you all know and understand your part.

Not only does Paul address this letter to the believers that lived in Ephesus, but he also addressed this letter to the believers that live in the surrounding communities. Paul had to convince the Christian believers who they were in CHRIST. Why do you think Paul would have to convince the believers who they were in CHRIST? I mean, what would be the reason to convince someone who they are in CHRIST?

One of the reasons is because Paul wanted to persuade the believers that through the believers CHRIST is completing what HE began when HE was here on earth. That's why Paul uses the analogy of us being The Church, The Body of CHRIST. As CHRIST's Body, we're supposed to operate as CHRIST did on earth. Not one particular individual to do the work that CHRIST did, but us coming together as CHRIST's Body to do the work that CHRIST did. That's why there's no big 'I's' or little 'u's.' When we are all a part of CHRIST's Body, we all have a part to play. No one is the Head but CHRIST. No one person can do all the work CHRIST did.

When we come together as a body of believers who represent CHRIST's Body, then through all of our gifts we should be able to finish the work HE started. The importance of every believer knowing what part they are supposed to be in The Body should tell them how important it is for them to play their part. Everybody in The Body of CHRIST has a part to play. If any part of The Body is not doing its part, then The Body becomes dysfunctional. If I have two legs, and one of them decides they don't want to get involved, it makes it harder for The Body to get from place to place. Either I have to learn how to hop, or another part of my body has to try to do what the leg decided it didn't want to do. Could you imagine my arm, which already has a responsibility, trying to do what it's responsible for and also trying to do what the leg is supposed to be doing?

The sad reality is, that's the problem in The Church; believers not wanting to get involved. This causes other believers to try to do their part they are not designed to do, which makes The Church become dysfunctional. Not only do we become dysfunctional, but we look dysfunctional. That's Paul's message to the Ephesians; the importance of everyone's body part being functional. Nobody's body part is to just come and receive the blessings GOD has to offer The Body and not be functional. Every believer has a part. And Paul wants us to realize that we are The Church. By us being The Church, we represent "CHRIST's Body!"

As CHRIST's Body, we're supposed to function like CHRIST. The only way The Church can function like CHRIST is, every believer has to do their part to make CHRIST's Body function. Paul tells us in Ephesians 4:1, I therefore, the prisoner of the Lord, beseech you that ye walk worthy of the vocation wherewith ye are called. A lot of people don't realize how important it is for each of us to walk in our calling. When we refuse to walk in our calling, it causes The Body to struggle in being effective.

You never want to be the cause of The Body not functioning properly. Sometimes, when a certain part of The Body is not functioning, the best thing to do is to cut it off. If it's not functioning, it's just in the way. If my arm is trying to walk for my leg, because my leg chooses not to, when people see me, they're not going to say, "Look at his leg being lazy." They're going to look at the whole body as being dysfunctional. It's better to learn how to hop than it is to keep carrying dead weight.

GOD Chose Us Through CHRIST
Verses 3-14

Because we represent CHRIST's Body, look at what Paul says in verse 3, Praise the GOD and Father of our Lord JESUS CHRIST! Through CHRIST, GOD has blessed us with every spiritual blessing that heaven has to offer. Everything heaven has to offer, GOD has blessed us with. There are benefits to being a part of The Body. If I eat healthily, my arm is not the only part of my body that benefits, my whole body benefits.

By being a part of The Body, Paul says, "GOD has blessed us with every spiritual blessing that heaven has to offer." He made sure he reminded the believers that these blessings that heaven gives us are only through CHRIST. So, if I try to detach myself from The Body of CHRIST, then I'm not entitled to the blessings that heaven has to offer The Body.

A lot of people try to take GOD's gifts that HE has equipped them with to work in The Body of CHRIST and then try to use them outside The Body of CHRIST. Then they wonder why they can't be successful in the world with the gift they're supposed to be using in The Body of CHRIST. Verse 3 tells us blessings that heaven has to offer only come through being connected to CHRIST. It's okay to go out into the world if you are still connected to CHRIST's Body. Because if you look through the Bible, CHRIST did most of HIS work outside The Church. The problem in The Church is we try to take GOD's gifts, separate ourselves from The Body, and then go out into the world. And then get mad at GOD because we're not being blessed. The text says, "Through CHRIST..., GOD has blessed us with every spiritual blessing that heaven has to offer.

In order for me to keep reaping the blessings that heaven has to offer, whether I'm inside or outside the building, I need to stay connected to The Body of CHRIST. If I disconnect myself from HIS Body, then I disconnect myself from the blessings that heaven has to offer. I only reap the blessings that heaven has to offer by being connected to CHRIST's Body. So, it's our job to make sure we stay connected to The Body.

After Paul tells us in verse 3, GOD blesses us with every spiritual blessing that heaven has to offer. Look at what Paul says next in verses 4-6, Before the creation of the world, HE chose us through CHRIST to be holy and perfect in HIS presence. Because of HIS love HE had already decided to adopt us through JESUS CHRIST. HE freely chose to do this so that the kindness HE had given us in HIS dear Son would be praised and given glory.

Did you see what Paul just said? Let's back up to verse 4. Paul says, Before the creation of the world, GOD chose us through CHRIST to be holy and perfect in HIS presence. So, the only way I can present myself in GOD's presence as holy and perfect is when I represent CHRIST's Body. Look at what the text says, the only way GOD chooses us is through CHRIST. By us being attached to CHRIST, we're supposed to present CHRIST's Body as holy and perfect in GOD's presence. Now could you imagine being the one that's making CHRIST's Body look dysfunctional before GOD's presence?

The only way GOD looks at us individually as holy and perfect is when we are attached to HIS Son CHRIST. Since I represent HIS Son by being attached to The Body, then I need to make sure I'm being effective in doing my part. When I choose not to do my part and The Body stands in GOD's presence, if my part is the arm and the arm is just dangling, then GOD looks at the arm and says, "What's wrong with CHRIST's Body." I never want to stand in the presence of GOD and be responsible for making CHRIST's Body look dysfunctional.

Verse 5 says the only reason GOD allows us to represent HIS Son as a body is because of HIS love for us. HE decided to adopt us through

JESUS CHRIST. The reason HE decided to adopt us is because of …the kindness HE had given us in HIS dear Son would be praised and given glory. When we are connected and being effective, it brings praise and glory to GOD. Whenever GOD sees us as a Body, we're supposed to represent praise and glory; not dysfunctional. Whenever GOD sees HIS Son, HE sees praise and glory. We are supposed to resemble HIS Son every time we come into HIS presence. The worst thing we can do, as a church, is be a bad representation of CHRIST's Body, especially in GOD's presence.

It's bad enough to be a bad representation of CHRIST's Body to the world, but it is even worse to be a bad representation of CHRIST's Body in GOD's presence. HE didn't give us HIS Son for us to make HIS Son look foolish and dysfunctional. Now, I understand why the Bible tells us to present our body as a living sacrifice, holy and acceptable. (Romans 12:1) When the world sees us, they are supposed to see a representation of what CHRIST looks like.

Imagine how it makes GOD feel when the world sees us, and they're laughing at us. If we represent CHRIST's Body, then when they laugh at us, they're laughing at what GOD sees as HIS Son CHRIST. I don't know about you, but I don't want to be the reason the world is laughing at the image of HIS Son. Again, this is why Paul opens this letter with letting believers know that he knows his part.

I understand why the Bible allows us to judge each other righteously. (John 7:24) Whenever I see a believer not resembling CHRIST, I'm supposed to judge them righteously and not according to my opinion. The only reason GOD allows us to judge one another and not the world, is, so we can go back to looking like the image of CHRIST. We are to assist one another in mimicking CHRIST.

Could you imagine if the whole Body of CHRIST looked identical to CHRIST? Not only would it bring praise and glory to GOD. Can you imagine all the spiritual blessings we would receive that heaven has to offer? If all of this seems like it's way too much, or way too much responsibility for us as believers, I'm glad Paul says what he says in verse 7. Through the blood of HIS Son, we are set free from our sins. GOD forgives our failures because of HIS overflowing kindness.

Trying to resemble CHRIST may be hard, but it's not impossible. Even when we fall short, Paul says, "GOD forgives our failures." So, every time we fail, as long as we are still attached to JESUS' Body, GOD doesn't see our failure, but HE sees HIS Son JESUS'. And what can wash away my sins? Through the blood of HIS Son, JESUS. And it's because of HIS blood that GOD forgives our sins.

GOD is not looking for us to be perfect. HE's just looking for our willingness to be a living sacrifice. When GOD sees me, because I have been covered by JESUS' blood, I look perfect and holy before HIM, because when GOD sees me, HE sees HIS Son JESUS. If every disciple presented themselves as a living sacrifice, not perfect, but holy and acceptable, then when GOD sees us, HE will see HIS Son JESUS. Then as a Body, we would receive everything heaven has to offer.

There are blessings that are promised to me, but then there are blessings that are promised to us as a body. It's only when we as a Body start resembling CHRIST, that we as a body will start receiving every blessing heaven has to offer. I don't know about you, but I want to reap every blessing that heaven has to offer. So, if I have to tell you the truth in order for you to start resembling CHRIST, then I'm willing to tell you the truth.

That's exactly why Paul is dealing with 'us in CHRIST' and not 'CHRIST in us,' like he did in Romans, Corinthians, and Galatians. Paul wants us to understand how important it is for us to be connected to The Body. And not only be connected to The Body, but be effective while we are connected. Now, watch what verses 8 and 9 tell us, HE poured out HIS kindness by giving us every kind of wisdom and insight when HE revealed the mystery HIS of plan to us. HE had decided to do this through CHRIST. I think the reason a lot of believers are not being effective in The Body is because they don't understand the importance of doing their part.

When you are attached to CHRIST's Body, and not a solo gig, GOD pours out and gives us wisdom and insight of HIS plan that HE only gives those who are attached to The Body. What did the end of verse 9 say? HE had decided to do this through CHRIST., which is The Body. So, whenever The Body resembles CHRIST, everything GOD gave to CHRIST, HE now gives to The Body that represents CHRIST.

GOD gives us wisdom and insight of HIS plan when we are connected to The Body. If I'm not receiving wisdom and insight, then I need to make sure I am connected to The Body. When we are not connected to The Body, then we start leaning to our own understanding. This is why it's important to be a part of a ministry that preaches and teaches GOD's Word, because when GOD gives us insight of HIS plan, HE gives us insight of HIS plan through HIS Word. Because Faith comes by hearing, hearing by the word of GOD. (2nd Corinthians 5:17)

Anytime you receive GOD's Word, by you being connected to The Body, HIS Word will always bring you wisdom, insight, revelation, and confirmation. To understand GOD's plan, you cannot lean to your own understanding. That's why Paul calls GOD's Word a mystery. (1 Corinthians 4:1) But when you are connected to The Body, Paul says, HE pours out every kind of wisdom and insight when HE reveals to us HIS plan or HIS will.

At the end of verse 9, Paul says the only way GOD reveals HIS plan is through CHRIST. The only way HE gives me the wisdom to understand HIS plan is, I must be connected to CHRIST. Why? HE only reveals HIS plans to The Body. Now, watch what Paul says in verse 10, HE (GOD) planned to bring all of history to its goal in CHRIST. Then CHRIST would be the Head of everything in heaven and on earth; all of heaven is on one accord. But the problem is that it becomes dysfunctional here on Earth. GOD intended for CHRIST to be the Head in heaven and here on earth. Heaven is on one accord, but why does Earth have to make HiIS Body dysfunctional? If CHRIST is the Head, and we represent The Body, could you imagine how CHRIST feels when we make HIS Body look dysfunctional?

If GOD's will is to be done here on Earth as it is in heaven, then it's important for us to be effective as a body. (Luke 11:9-13) It's not supposed to be perfect in heaven and jacked-up on Earth. They are not supposed to be on one accord in heaven, but we're fighting each other here on Earth. The model prayer in Matthew 6:10 says, YOUR will be done on Earth as it is in heaven. The only way GOD's will can be done on Earth as it is in Heaven is for believers to come together on one accord and finish the work that CHRIST started. I mean, what would you think if you saw someone fighting themselves? You would think they are crazy because that's dysfunctional. Well, how do you think The Church looks to the world when The Body of CHRIST is fighting against itself? The exact same way; crazy and dysfunctional.

GOD established CHRIST as the Head. HE never intended for CHRIST to have a dysfunctional body. Paul says to the Ephesians in verse 11, GOD also decided ahead of time to choose us through CHRIST according to HIS plan, which makes everything work the way HE intends. It's in GOD's plan that everything works the way HE intended; never for The Body to be dysfunctional. That's why I stated earlier, I do not want to be the cause or the reason for CHRIST's Body being dysfunctional. When we make HIS Body dysfunctional, it's no longer presentable in GOD's presence.

Do you know how many ministries GOD doesn't allow to come into HIS presence, because HE can't reveal HIS plan through HIS Word? Anytime you compromise GOD's Word, you have just made CHRIST's

Body dysfunctional. GOD's Word is life to The Body of CHRIST. If there is no life, then GOD is not revealing HIS plan. If GOD can't reveal HIS plan through HIS Word, then HE stops pouring out wisdom and insight for us to understand the mysteries of HIS plan.

In verse 12, Paul states, HE planned all of this so that we who had already focused our hope on CHRIST would praise HIM and give HIM glory. But how can The Body bring HIM praise and glory when The Body is dysfunctional? How can The Body bring GOD praise and glory, when it's not even presentable to be in HIS presence? We must make sure we present CHRIST's Body as holy and perfect by presenting our body as a living sacrifice in HIS presence.

I will always present my body as a sacrifice by doing my part in The Body. When you make yourself a living sacrifice, it's standing before GOD telling HIM, "Whatever YOU want me to do in The Body, I'm willing to sacrifice my body to do it. Even if I don't want to go, I'm willing to make the sacrifice. Even if I have to drive across town, I'm willing to make the sacrifice. Whatever it takes to make CHRIST's Body not to be dysfunction-al, I'm willing to make the sacrifice."

Now, let's look at verses 13 and 14, You heard and believed the message of truth, the Good News that HE has saved you. In HIM, you were sealed with the HOLY SPIRIT whom HE promised. This HOLY SPIRIT is the guarantee that we will receive our inheritance. We have this guarantee until we are set free to belong to him. GOD receives praise and glory for this. Once again, Paul reminds us that even though it may be a sacrifice, we always have help. And who does Paul say our Help is? The HOLY SPIRIT.

Not only is the HOLY SPIRIT our help to make CHRIST's Body presentable in GOD's presence, but look at what Paul says in verse 14, The HOLY SPIRIT is our guarantee that we will receive our inheritance. So, everything heaven has to offer, the HOLY SPIRIT will make sure we receive it. In other words, GOD will always do HIS part. We must make sure we do ours; making CHRIST's Body acceptable in GOD's presence by doing our individual part.

Once GOD sees The Body resembling HIS Son, then HE tells heaven to release every blessing heaven has to offer. And it is my prayer that you want every blessing that heaven has to offer, not only the blessings heaven has for you individually, but even the blessings heaven has for us as a Body. One may ask, why would GOD establish imperfect people to be an extension of a perfect Savior? Because honestly, the reason The Church has so many problems is because of the imperfect people that make up The Body. As imperfect as The Church may be, GOD made it perfectly clear that HE has chosen The Church to bring HIS message of love and salvation to a hurting world.

The reason GOD establishes imperfect people to be an extension of a perfect Savior is because GOD decided to use hurt imperfect people to help save a hurt imperfect world. That's exactly why ministry should be important to every believer. We who are now The Body of CHRIST should be able to relate to their hurt and know how to minister to the hurt. Why? Because we have experienced it.

Now watch this, CHRIST decided to go to the cross and die for a world HE did not know how to relate to by experience. CHRIST didn't know what it felt like to fall short to sin because HE never sinned. But yet, HE died for our sins. HE took on sin, but HE never experienced sinning. And most of the stuff CHRIST had to endure came at the end of HIS ministry. Yet, HE was willing to pay a price HE did not owe because we had a debt we couldn't pay.

So, ministry should never be a bother to us, as believers, because we know how it feels to fall short. We know how it feels to disappoint GOD. Yet, we judge people when they disappoint GOD. Every time we come together as believers, our main goal should always be to save someone from going to hell, because now we can relate to that at one time, we were on our way to hell also. Oh, but GOD!

The only way for us to operate the same way CHRIST did, when HE was here on Earth, is that we must come together as one Body. I can't do the work CHRIST did by myself, but we can if we come together as one body. It's going to take us coming together to do the work that CHRIST did Through all of our gifts together, we should be able to finish the work that CHRIST started. The Church doesn't have time to be fighting itself because we should be more focused on trying to finish the work that CHRIST started.

Everything GOD gave to CHRIST to do, HE now gives to The Body. The reason GOD gives us everything HE gave CHRIST is because when CHRIST came to Earth, HE fulfilled GOD's will in Heaven here on Earth. When CHRIST left, GOD needed HIS will on Earth to be fulfilled. It's our job to now fulfill GOD's will on Earth as it is in Heaven. We can't fulfill HIS will on Earth if The Body is dysfunctional.

The only way GOD can reveal HIS plan in Heaven here on Earth is through the believers that come together as CHRIST's Body. That's why it's important for us to stay connected to The Body. When Paul prayed for the Ephesians in the beginning of the letter to them, he wanted believers to understand the importance of us being The Body of CHRIST. HIS prayer for the believers in chapter 1 is so the believers can understand that all the power they need, they already have in GOD. Their Faith determines how much power is released.

A lot of times in our prayers, we ask GOD for more blessings, power, or more whatever. But when we ask GOD for more power or more blessings, who is the source of the power, and who is the source of the blessings? GOD, right? Well, if GOD is in me, I have all the power I need inside of me. If GOD is the source of my blessings, I have every blessing already inside of me. We just need to know how to tap into the power inside of us. We have no reason to ask GOD for more power, as if there is more power outside of GOD.

If GOD is all-powerful and HE dwells inside of us, then we have all the power GOD has inside of us. We just have to learn how to tap into that power by Faith that we already have inside. GOD is the source, and all power is in GOD. It's our Faith that determines how much of GOD we release.

The reason we find Paul praying for the believers in chapter 1 is so the believers can understand that all the power they need, they already have in GOD. Their Faith determines how much power is released. We don't need to ask GOD for more. We just need to increase our level of Faith for HIM to release more.

Paul's Prayer for the Ephesians
Verses 15-23

So, very quickly, let's look at Paul's prayer to the Ephesians. Ephesians 1:15-17, I, too, have heard about your Faith in the Lord JESUS and your love for all of GOD's people. For this reason, I never stop thanking GOD for you. I always remember you in my prayers. I pray that the glorious FATHER, the GOD of our Lord JESUS CHRIST, would give you a spirit of wisdom and revelation as you come to know CHRIST better.

Paul says, you have Faith in GOD, and for that, I am proud of you. But it is my prayer that you get to know GOD better, through CHRIST. We can't miss Paul's emphasis 'through CHRIST.' You can't receive what GOD has to offer being detached from The Body of CHRIST. GOD doesn't give everything HE has to offer through one person, but HE gives all HE has to offer through The Body.

Paul tells the Ephesians, all of you are operating in Faith, but the things you're going to have to deal with, you're going to have to increase your Faith to release more of GOD's power. Watch what Paul says in verse 17, I pray you come to know CHRIST better. See, you all have the Faith to release power to get over your stumbling blocks. But, y'all have not tapped into the power to get rid of your mountains. None of you have elevated your Faith to release power to defeat demonic warfare. To be able to deal with certain warfare, you're not going to be able to defeat it by limiting GOD's power based on where your level of Faith is.

Paul tells them, I need you to get more familiar with what you already have inside of you. Because once you understand that you have everything inside of you, the more you increase your level of Faith, the more of GOD you release into the atmosphere. Paul says in verses 18 and 19, Then you will have deeper insight. You will know the confidence that HE calls you to have and the glorious wealth that GOD's people will inherit. You will also know the unlimited greatness of HIS power as it works with might and strength for us, the believers. The problem is not that you don't have Faith. The problem is, you are limiting GOD with your level of Faith. So, there are parts of GOD that you have yet to tap into.

Once you get to know CHRIST better, Then you will have deeper insight, and you will know the unlimited greatness of HIS power as it works with might and strength for us. Watch this, the believers. That was so powerful! Paul is saying, when you know the strength that GOD gives us, once we are aware of all the parts of The Body and what they are used for, we then become a force to be reckoned with.

Once The Body realizes what all the other body parts are capable of doing with the help of the HOLY SPIRIT, then The Body doesn't have to waste unnecessary energy doing stuff it's not supposed to be doing. It can focus on what GOD has equipped it to do and be effective. Once each part starts doing their part, you will know the unlimited greatness of HIS power as it works! (Verse 19)

The more we come together as a body, the more GOD can release HIS power through The Body. When we stop seeing miracles and blessings being released through The Body, it's because we are limiting GOD's power as a Body. That's why it's important for everybody to do their part in The Body. We limit GOD's power, when we don't do our part. When GOD's powers are limited, then miracles, blessings, signs, and wonders are limited. All of GOD's power will never come through one individual, but the totality of GOD's powers is released when the believers come together as a Body.

Paul tells us in verses 20 and 21 the authority of CHRIST. HE worked with that same power in CHRIST when HE brought him back to life and gave him the highest position in Heaven. HE is far above all rulers, authorities, powers, lords, and all other names that can be named, not only in this present world but also in the world to come. CHRIST is far above all of these other powers and authorities, and we represent The Body of CHRIST. We are to operate in the same authority that GOD gave CHRIST when HE raised HIM from the dead. We are to be the exact replica of CHRIST's Body. To back up what Paul just said, GOD's will is to be done here on Earth as it is in Heaven, look at what Paul says in verse 20, GOD has given CHRIST the highest position in Heaven.

CHRIST has the highest position in Heaven, The Body of CHRIST is to have the highest position here on Earth. We can't hold the highest position on Earth when we limit GOD's powers as a body. The Body of CHRIST needs to decide to walk in the authority that GOD has given us as a body here on Earth.

Paul closes out chapter 1 in verses 22 and 23, GOD has put everything under the control of CHRIST. HE has made CHRIST the Head of everything for the good of The Church. The Church is CHRIST's Body and completes HIM as HE fills everything in every way. Now, it doesn't get any plainer than that. Paul said, GOD has put everything under the control of CHRIST," for the good of The Church.

HE didn't put everything under the control of the pastor.
HE didn't put everything under the control of the bishops.
HE didn't put everything under the control of the apostles
or the prophets.

In order for me to operate in the same authority that has been given to CHRIST, I need to be connected to The Body. The same authority that GOD has given me through CHRIST, is now given to us as a Body. Look at verse 23, The Church is CHRIST's Body and completes HIM as HE fills everything in every way. Paul says as believers, because we represent CHRIST's Body, we're to complete HIM. We can't complete HIM if The Body is dysfunctional and individually we are absent from The Body. The only way CHRIST can fulfill everything in every way is, The Church has to come together as CHRIST's Body.

Chapter 2

God's Power

GOD Saved Us Because of His Great Love for Us
Verses 1-10

As The Body, GOD has given us everything we need to function properly. One person can't do it all, no matter how powerful their gift is. Side note: If anyone tries to take the place of the Head, CHRIST, it is a cult. When one person tries to do every function of The Body, they get burnt out in ministry because they end up carrying all the weight of the ministry when the weight is supposed to be distributed amongst all the believers. That's why I could never understand why some people say, "You don't have to go to church." You can't receive this type of wisdom, revelation, and greatness by sitting at home; but by coming together as a body.

Now, as we enter into Ephesians chapter 2, Paul wants the Ephesians to understand how powerful GOD is, and without GOD, how powerless we are. A lot of believers don't know how to tap into the power they have. We end up being powerless as a Body, not realizing that the trick of the enemy is to make us think we don't have the power we already possess. If you have a weapon, and I know you're not going to use it, you are not a threat to me just because you have a weapon. The Church doesn't become a threat to the enemy or demonic warfare just because we have the HOLY SPIRIT. When the enemy knows we're not going to tap into the power of the HOLY SPIRIT, then he knows there is not a threat towards him. What good is it to have all this power available, if we're not going to tap into it? What good is it to come together, if we're not going to reap the benefits of coming together?

But when we choose not to tap into the power of God, all we're doing is jumping and shouting with an emotional high. GOD didn't give The Church power for us to jump and shout, but HE gave us power to perform signs and wonders. Because honestly, I can jump and shout without power. I don't know about you, but I don't want to come out of warfare feeling good and victorious. I don't want to go into battle with the enemy and come out feeling good. Furthermore, I want to defeat the enemy because of the power I decided to tap into. So, the next time he even thinks about trying me, he knows he's in for the fight of his life. There's no way in the world, I'm going to have access to omnipotent power and not tap into it. That's the problem with The Church Body, we have access to an almighty GOD, but we refuse to tap into HIS power.

In verse 1 Paul says, You were once dead because of your failures and your sins. You followed the ways of this present world and its spiritual ruler. This ruler continues to work in the people who refuse to obey GOD. Because of our sins, we were dead. Dead is a strong word. Paul could have said, because of your sins, you were nothing. Even if I have nothing, at least I still exist. With Paul using the word dead, it was as if you did not even exist. The person GOD created you to be, because of your failures and sins, that person died.

Here's how your sins destroy who GOD created you to be. Paul says in verse 2, You followed the ways of the world and its spiritual ruler. This ruler still continues to work in people who refuse to obey GOD. The worst thing someone could do is to be in church and disobey GOD by still following the ways of the world. It doesn't do you any good to be in church if you're not going to be in CHRIST. There's no way I can be in CHRIST and still be following the ways of the world. Remember, what Romans 6:1-2 tells, What shall we say then? Shall we continue in sin, that grace may abound? GOD forbid. How shall we, that are dead to sin, live any longer therein?

According to the text, when I choose to follow the ways of the world and its spiritual ruler, it causes me to disobey GOD. My disobedience causes me to sin, and sin destroys who GOD created me to be. Matthew 6:34 makes a lot of sense; no one can serve two masters: for either he will hate one and love the other. No one can be a follower of CHRIST and still choose to follow the ways of the world and its spiritual ruler. Why? There's no way to follow two masters. You can't be a follower of both.

Verse 3 tells us, All of us once lived among these people and followed the desires of our corrupt nature. We did what our corrupt desires and thoughts wanted us to do. So, because of our nature, we deserved GOD's anger just like everyone else. Whenever we follow our corrupt nature, it angers GOD. You can't please GOD and anger HIM at the same time. And you definitely can't please GOD following your corrupt nature. If our corrupt nature causes us to sin against GOD, and our sins destroy who GOD created us to be, do you know how many people are in The Church that are dead because of their sins? Just being in The Church does not make you a Christian, just like standing in the garage doesn't make you a car.

Let's look at verses 4 and 5, But GOD is rich in mercy because of HIS great love for us. We were dead because of our failures, but HE made us alive together with CHRIST. (It is GOD's grace that saved you.) Because GOD loves us, HE gave and gives us grace and mercy. Once GOD's grace and mercy saved us, it brought us back to life. It is found in verses 6 and 7 the reason GOD allows grace and mercy to give us life, GOD has brought us back to life together with CHRIST JESUS and has given us a position in heaven with him. HE did this through CHRIST JESUS out of HIS generosity to us in order to show HIS extremely rich kindness in the world to come.

Paul lets us know GOD brings us back to life so that we can sit in authority with CHRIST. This is another important reason we are to represent CHRIST as a Body. Here's why you can't attach something that is dead to something that's living. Could you imagine a healthy body and the whole arm is dead? Everybody that's in The Church building is not necessarily attached to The Church Body. The only way to be attached to The Church Body is, you have to first be in CHRIST.

Everything that's attached to CHRIST is living and useful. We just have to make sure it's being used. You can have something that is useful and still not use it. You can have a $2 million car sitting in the garage and never drive it. Sidenote: Have you ever been driving on the freeway, and see a little old person driving a $200,000 car? I say to myself, they're just driving that car because they have money. All the gadgets that come with that car goes to waste because all they know how to do is start and drive it. It's very easy to have something that's useful and not use it.

When something is dead, it will never be useful. Here's where The Church makes its mistake, just because someone is in The Church building, we try to attach them to The Church Body. If they are dead, they end up doing more damage to The Body. Until GOD allows grace and mercy to bring back to life that which was dead, then we shouldn't try to attach them to The Body. I don't care how good they can work, sing, or preach. If they have not been saved by grace and mercy, they are still dead because of their sins.

That's the reason GOD doesn't allow us to inherit salvation through our works. This is explained in verses 8 and 9, For by grace you have been saved through Faith, and that not of yourselves; it is the gift of GOD, not of works, lest anyone should boast. GOD says salvation is a gift through Faith. If we could work for it, we would boast about how we got it. We will start feeling like, just because I do more work than you, then I am more saved than you. In other words, the more work I do, the more saved I am.

Paul tells us that before we start bragging about how we got salvation, GOD gave it to us as a free gift. So, one person's gift is no greater than another gift. So, grace examines our Faith through our confession, determines what we believe, and evaluates if what comes out of our mouth is also in our hearts. The Bible says in Matthew 7:21, not every-one that says Lord Lord will enter into the kingdom of heaven. Even though some people may say it, it doesn't mean they mean it.

Based on the results of our Faith, grace determines if we receive the free gift of salvation. Once we receive the gift of salvation, it then gives us life in The Body of CHRIST. That which was dead now has life because of CHRIST. After we receive life in CHRIST, verse 10 tells us, For we are HIS workmanship, created in CHRIST JESUS for good works, which GOD prepared beforehand that we should walk in them. We don't work for salvation, we work after we receive salvation. The reason we are required to work after salvation is that now, we are equipped to work. Now, we are useful to The Body because Faith without works is dead. Now, we are no longer dead because of sin, but now we are alive because of CHRIST.

We are more useful to The Body of CHRIST alive than we are dead. Anything that's dead needs to be buried and not attached to The Body of CHRIST, until it's ready to receive life. Only that which has life is useful to The Body. It's dangerous to forsake the assembly of The Body by being absent. According to Paul, there are some things GOD only releases when The Body comes together on one accord. What we don't realize a lot of times is, there's power in unity. Especially, in The Body of CHRIST. The Church only becomes a threat to the enemy, when we know how to tap into the authority that GOD has given us through the HOLY SPIRIT. If we have the HOLY SPIRIT dwelling on the inside of us, then we should be a threat to demonic warfare and spiritual wickedness that sits in high places.

I should be a threat to the enemy all by myself. Why? I have learned how to tap into the authority that GOD has put on the inside of me. But, could you imagine the kind of threat The Church would be if all believ-ers would come together and tap into that same authority? All kinds of miracles would take place. When GOD's Word is going forth, then GOD is going forth. Remember what Paul told us in Ephesians 1:19, Then you will know the unlimited greatness of HIS power as it works with might and strength for us, which are the believers. Whenever GOD is going forth, we need to make sure we are present in The Body and not absent from The Body. I can't tap into this type of greatness if I am absent.

Paul has been teaching us the importance of us coming together as a Body. But not just coming together, but being effective when we are together. In order for us to be effective, we all have to play a part. There are a lot of believers that come together as a Body but are not effective when they come together. You can have GOD's power available and not access it. You can have something that's useful and not use it. Our job as believers is to make sure that what GOD has provided for The Body is being used.

Well, if Paul's main focus is The Church being The Body of CHRIST, what would Paul's main message to the believer be? Unity. When we're not in unity, we make The Body dysfunctional. Paul has been showing us through the book of Ephesians that GOD's plan is to unite all things in CHRIST as One Body. If GOD's plan is to unite us as One Body, then why is there so much division in The Body of CHRIST?

In the next few verses, Paul deals with the division and hostility that existed between the Jews and the Gentiles. During this time, a lot of the Jews thought JESUS only came back to save them. What the Jews forgot was, when GOD made a promise to Abraham and his descendants, GOD wasn't only trying to save Abraham's seeds. HIS goal was to save mankind through the promise HE made to Abraham and his seeds.

GOD was never trying to establish a race of people. HIS desire was to establish a Faith of people. Through Faith, they would be saved, not because of their race. The Bible never said GOD sent HIS Son to die for the Jews. The Bible says in John 3:16 (KJV), For GOD so loved the world, that HE gave HIS only begotten SON, that whosoever believeth in HIM should not perish, but have everlasting life.

Paul talked about how GOD united Jewish and non-Jewish people, based on unity in The Body of CHRIST. In all reality, The Body of CHRIST is one of the most divided belief systems there is. Even with this being said, Whites don't want to fellowship with Blacks, Asians don't want to fellowship with Latinos, but we are all supposed to be representing One Body of CHRIST.

GOD Has United Jewish & Non-Jewish People
Verses 11-22

Look what Paul says to the Ephesians in verses 11-13, Remember that once you were not Jewish physically. Those who called themselves 'the circumcised' because of what they had done to their bodies called you 'the uncircumcised.' Also, at that time you were without CHRIST. You were excluded from citizenship in Israel, and the pledges (GOD made in HIS) promise were foreign to you. You had no hope and were in the world without GOD. But now through CHRIST JESUS you, who were once far away, have been brought near by the blood of CHRIST.

Paul tells us in these verses that before we accepted CHRIST, we belonged to different races. But, because we are all saved by the same blood, we're all a part of one family. Once you become a follower of CHRIST, you become family by Faith. When you become a part of this family, there are no more races, only Christians. We are all one family. We were all saved by the same blood. Same blood, one family. When you belong to GOD's family, you don't represent a race of people. You represent a Faith of people. GOD doesn't see race. HE just sees humanity.

When Satan was going to and fro, GOD asked Satan, Hast thou considered my servant Job, ..." (Job 2:3 KJV) GOD didn't identify Job based on anything other than being a servant. GOD didn't say, Job and Satan had to ask HIM, "Which one? The Latino one?" No! Satan knew who Job was based on him being a servant, not a Jew or Gentile, but a servant.

Let's look at verse 12 again, ...before you accepted CHRIST, you were without hope and a promise. You weren't without hope because you weren't a Jew, you were without hope because you didn't have CHRIST. Sidenote: Anyone who tries to make you feel that GOD does not accept you because you are not a part of their religion is a cult. GOD is not a religion, HE is a relationship. The relationship that GOD establishes through Faith is the relationship between a Father and a child. That's why when we become believers, HE makes us one in CHRIST. HE only had one begotten Son. HE didn't have a Latino son and an Asian daughter, and a black son, and a white daughter.

John 3:16 says, HE gave us HIS only begotten Son. That's why, when we present ourselves to HIM as One Body. When HE sees us, HE is supposed to see HIS son. Not a body with a black arm, a white leg, an Asian shoulder, or a Latino hip. We've all been saved by the same blood, that should make us one in CHRIST. There shouldn't be a clique over here and a clique over there, not if we are all under the same blood.

If there are different groups in The Church, it's because somebody is not saved by the same blood. This is explained in verse 14, So HE is our peace. In HIS Body, HE has made Jewish and non-Jewish people one by breaking down the wall of hostility that kept them apart. For those who are under the same blood, it's easy for them to get along. It's easy for them to come together on one accord because HE is our peace. In HIM, we are the same and the walls of hostility have been destroyed.

So, people who like to keep up mess in The Church and cause division are probably not saved by His blood. To back up what he just said in verse 14, that there is no division amongst the believers. Look at what Paul says in verses 15 and 16: HE brought an end to the commandments and demands found in Moses' Teachings so that HE could take Jewish and non-Jewish people and create one new humanity in himself. So, HE made peace. HE also brought them back to GOD in One Body by His cross, on which HE killed the hostility. So, hatred towards your brother and sister was destroyed on the cross.

Even if I don't get along with my own family, I should always get along with my family in CHRIST. Even if we have a disagreement, it shouldn't separate us; the peace we have in CHRIST will always bring us back to GOD in One Body. Because Can two walk together, except they agree? (Amos 3:3) We have become One Body through the blood of CHRIST. Eventually, we're going to be able to touch and agree on the same thing.

Whatever we are confused about, the moment we come together as One Body, verse 17 tells us, then GOD will give you a spirit of wisdom and revelation as you come to know CHRIST better. So, whatever we were confused about that made us disagree, when we come together, GOD will give us wisdom and revelation so that we can be on one accord. I can guarantee again that if two of you agree on anything here on earth, my Father in heaven will accept it. Where two or three have come together in my name, I am there among them. (Matthew 18:19-20) Whenever CHRIST shows up, confusion must go. Whenever CHRIST shows up, The peace we have in CHRIST will always bring us back to GOD in one body.

Not only will the peace we have in CHRIST bring us back to GOD in One Body. But, look what Paul says in verses 17 and 18, He came with the Good News of peace for you who were far away and for those who were near. So Jewish and non-Jewish people can go to the Father in one SPIRIT. We can't be divided if we both have the same ONE Spirit. So, when CHRIST shows up in the midst of them that touch and agree, HE comes with peace to get rid of confusion in order for us to be able to go to GOD in one SPIRIT. Now, I don't know why a lot of preachers have you talk to your neighbor. But, I will have you talk to your neighbor so you both can agree. That way CHRIST can come in the midst and both of you are able to go to GOD in one SPIRIT. GOD dwells where there is unity and not division. If we are one family under the same SPIRIT, then it should be easy for us to come together on one accord.

Verse 19 states, That is why you are no longer foreigners and outsiders but citizens together with GOD's people and members of GOD's family. The only person you should have a problem not talking to or agreeing with is someone who is not under the same blood. So, in actuality, if we are saved by the same blood which makes us family, it shouldn't be, "tell your neighbor," but it should be, "tell your family." A neighbor is someone who is outside the family.

Paul closes Ephesians 2 with verses 20 – 22, You are built on the foundation of the apostles and prophets. CHRIST JESUS himself is the cornerstone. In HIM all the parts of the building fit together and grow into a holy temple in the Lord. Through HIM you, also, are being built in the SPIRIT together with others into a place where GOD lives.

The believers are truly built on a solid foundation, with CHRIST being the cornerstone, there's no way we can be a family in CHRIST and also be a divided body. In CHRIST, all the parts of the building fit together and grow into a holy temple in the Lord.

Chapter 3

Prisoner of Christ

Paul's Work of Spreading the Good News
Verses 1-13

Now, before we enter chapter 3, let's recap some of the things we've already discussed. Paul has been dealing with is that it takes all our gifts coming together for us to be effective as a Body. When we don't come together in unity, it makes The Body of CHRIST dysfunctional. It's hard to be effective as a ministry when the body is dysfunctional. For us to do the work that CHRIST did, it takes all of us coming together as one. The more we come together, the more effective we can be. What most people don't realize is, the more we come together, as believers, the more GOD can release HIS power through The Body. When The Body is dysfunctional, it limits the power GOD is able to release through the body.

That's why I believe in all the gifts of the Spirit. Each gift is GOD's way of operating through The Body. We never want to limit GOD from operating through The Body. The trick of the enemy is to make us think we don't have the power we already have in our possession. When we don't realize our power, we are no longer a threat to the enemy. What good is it for The Church to have GOD's power available to us, if we're not going to tap into the power HE has given us to operate as a body?

You should be a threat to the enemy all by yourself. Imagine the kind of threat The Church would be if all the believers would come together and tap into the authority that GOD has given us? Remember what Paul told us in Ephesians 1:19 Then, you will know the unlimited greatness of HIS power as it works through the believers. So, the believers, who represent

The Church, are to be operating in the unlimited greatness of GOD's power.

A lot of people only come to church looking for their breakthrough in deliverance, instead of coming together as a body, so the blessings can fall on everybody. What The Church needs to realize is, there's power in unity, not division or a solo act, but unity! There are some things GOD only releases when the body comes together. That's why every time we come together as a body; each person should always try to tap into everything that heaven has to offer. If you are empty, it was nobody's fault but yours. That's just wasted power! Even though the power is available, everybody doesn't choose to tap into it. Do you know how much power is wasted on the day of worship because people would rather come to church to feel good than to tap into everything heaven has to offer?

Now, when we enter chapter 3, we see Paul addressing the Christians in Ephesus from jail. Paul says in verse 1, This is the reason I, Paul, am the prisoner of CHRIST JESUS for those of you who are not Jewish. Paul starts off verse 1 by saying he was a prisoner for CHRIST; not metaphorically but literally. He was actually in prison when he wrote this letter. Paul is saying to the readers, because I am a prisoner of CHRIST, my assignment is to preach The Gospel to the world, and not just to the Jews. Instead of Paul complaining about his situation, he said, I glory in it because I am a prisoner for CHRIST. In other words, what I'm going through is because of ministry and not because I did anything wrong. When you are excited about doing ministry, you don't mind dealing with the outcome from ministry.

A lot of people don't realize what some of us have to give up or go through to do ministry. But, when you know what you're going through and what you are dealing with is because of ministry, it helps you to deal with the outcome of ministry.While Paul was writing this letter to the Christian believers, even being in prison, Paul was excited. Look at what Paul says in verses 2-4 Certainly, you have heard how GOD gave me the responsibility of bringing HIS kindness to you. You have heard that HE let me know this mystery through a revelation. I've already written to you about this briefly. When you read this, you'll see that I understand the mystery about CHRIST. He felt privileged because he had been chosen by GOD to reveal GOD's secret plan to man.

In verse 5 he says, In the past, this mystery was not known by people as it is now. The SPIRIT has now revealed it to HIS holy apostles and prophets. Assignments aren't given to everybody, just those who GOD has chosen. Watch the seriousness of Paul's statement. Paul says this information that is a mystery must be revealed because GOD does not give it to everybody to know. HE only gives this information to those HE can trust. If GOD gives me this information that's a mystery because HE can trust me, then imagine how it makes GOD feel if I misuse the information HE has given me. Imagine the consequences of not handling this information properly. Imagine not sharing the information that GOD has revealed.

What is this information that was a mystery, that GOD gave Paul that HE didn't give to everybody else? Verse 6 says, This mystery is the Good News that people who are not Jewish have the same inheritance as Jewish people do. They belong to the same body and share the same promise that GOD made in CHRIST JESUS. Everybody can be saved, not just the Jews. Anybody who accepts CHRIST becomes a part of The Body of CHRIST.

Now, suppose Paul said, "I don't want to upset the Jews. I'm going to change the information just so I can be accepted by the Jews, so I won't be talked about by other people, or so I can pack the pews. Telling the information as GOD gave it to me might put me in jail, or cause people not to like me." Well, where was Paul? In jail. So, evidently, the information Paul shared, was the information GOD revealed to him because where did Paul end up? In jail.

Paul said I didn't go to jail for doing something wrong. I went to jail for doing something right. I wasn't lied on because I did something wrong. I was lied on because I spoke about CHRIST. I'm not in this situation because I was being messy. I'm in the situation because GOD knew HE could trust me.

There are two things that happen when you know GOD can trust you. The first thing is you know how to count what you're going through as joy. The reason you're going through it is because of your assignment. That's why Paul said in verse 1 the reason I'm not tripping about being in prison is because of what I was called to do for CHRIST.

The second thing that happens when you know GOD can trust you is, you're not afraid of the outcome of your assignment. The reason GOD chose Paul was because most people would have said if "I knew this was going to put me in jail, I would have kept my mouth shut." GOD said, "Let ME reveal this assignment to someone who won't be afraid of the outcome of what I have called them to do. Let ME reveal this assignment to someone who won't be afraid to preach the Good News to the Gentiles, even though I know the Jews are not going to like it. Paul let ME reveal this assignment to you!"

Paul states in verse 7, I became a servant of this Good News through GOD's kindness freely given to me when HIS power worked in me. Paul says I became a servant to my assignment. And because GOD could trust me with the assignment, when HE gave it to me, HIS power began to work through me. Paul wants them to understand in verse 7 as the gift of the grace of GOD was given to me, HIS power began to work through me.

When Paul said, HIS power began to work through me, Paul said 'me' as singular. Look at what Paul says in verse 8. Paul goes on to say And I am the least of all the saints. When Paul said I am the least of all the saints, what he was saying was, and if GOD is able to do all of this through me, then what is The Church as a whole scared of. The only way to be able for GOD's power to work through you, is because verse 7 says the gift of the Good News was given to us through GOD's kindness. Then Paul continues to say HIS power began to work through you.

I know Paul is referencing all of this to The Church because look what

Paul says in verses 9-10, HE allowed me to explain the way this mystery works. GOD, who created all things, kept it hidden in the past. HE did this so that now, through The Church, HE could let the rulers and authorities in heaven know his infinite wisdom. That was powerful! Paul said individually, I was called to speak to the Gentiles, but as a body, we're supposed to be, not only speaking to nations, but we have the authority to speak to spiritual wickedness and principalities in high places.

The reason spiritual wickedness in high places is not afraid of The Church Body is because The Church doesn't know how to come together and allow HIS power to begin to work through us as a body. We are too concerned about getting emotionally aroused than we are about tapping into the power that can bring down strongholds. We are too concerned about what people are going to say and not offend people. GOD is not going to reveal HIS mysteries for us to turn around and figure out how we can change what HE said so we don't offend people. When GOD reveals HIS mysteries to us, it's not our job to try and understand the mysteries GOD revealed. Verse 10 explains this, ...so that through The Church, GOD could let principalities in high places know HIS infinite wisdom. Not what we have figured out ourselves.

If GOD gives me a word of knowledge regarding someone's situation, it's not up to me to try to figure out what their situation is. My job is to tell them exactly what GOD said. They will know it was GOD. Not because I tried to explain it to them or because I figured it out, but because I will say exactly what HE told me to tell them and they will know that it was GOD.

Some prophets today, they try to figure out what GOD has revealed to them by asking you questions. If GOD has given you a word to give to me, why are you asking me questions? Just give me what GOD said. If GOD said it, I would know HE said it. If 'you' add to what GOD said, either you're going to confuse what GOD said or you're going to say something GOD didn't say. A half truth is a whole lie. Can I get an amen?

Paul says in verse 11, This was GOD's plan for all of history which HE carried out through CHRIST JESUS our Lord. It has always been GOD's plan. HE just needed The Church to carry out HIS assignment. That's why I can only do so much by myself. But when we come together as a body, verse 10 says through The Church, GOD can let principalities in high places know HIS infinite wisdom. When The Church is silent, then principalities in high places don't know GOD's infinite wisdom, which causes them to start passing laws that go against GOD's plan.

The Church doesn't have to be silent, verse 12 says, We can go to GOD with bold confidence through Faith in CHRIST. As a matter of fact, the New King James Version says we have access. The Church doesn't have to be afraid to let principalities in high places know GOD's infinite wisdom when HE has given us access and authority.

Then after Paul tells The Church We can go to GOD with bold confidence through Faith in CHRIST, he says in verse 13, So then, I ask you not to become discouraged by the troubles I suffer for you. In fact, my troubles bring you glory. We don't have to be discouraged by the suffering the assignment is going to bring, because eventually, our assignment will bring us glory.

Paul Prays That GOD Would Strengthen Christians
Verses 14-21

One thing we have been discussing in chapter three is, when we don't realize our power, we stop being a threat to the enemy. Demonic spirits should never feel comfortable in church. Especially among believers who consider themselves saved. When we come together as The Body, we have an unlimited greatness of GOD's power. But, demonic spirits are not intimidated by us because we don't know how to tap into GOD's power as a Church Body.

What we need to realize, as The Church, there's power in unity. Every time The Body comes together on one accord, GOD is going to make sure The Body has everything it needs to operate. It's our job as believers to make sure what GOD has provided for The Body is being used. Make sure you don't forget what Paul has been telling us, it's an unlimited amount of power. This power doesn't run out. There's not a situation that can defeat this type of power because Paul said it's unlimited.

Not only have we been given unlimited power to perform signs and miracles, it was given to us to let spiritual wickedness know HIS infinite wisdom; not to run and hide. A lot of people change GOD's infinite wisdom so they can be popular. Others don't give you all of GOD's information HE gives them because they don't want to be offensive. But, when you consider yourself a prisoner of CHRIST, like Paul did, you don't mind dealing with the outcome from sharing GOD's infinite wisdom.

Now, I understand why the Bible says, woe unto the shepherds who destroy and scatter the sheep (Jeremiah 23:1). GOD says, "I have trusted you with this assignment. But because you don't want to deal with the outcome of the assignment, you're going to change up what I said. If you're not going to say what I have already said, then you should have never accepted the call. So, woe unto the one that leads my sheep astray!

The moment we decide to mishandle the gift that GOD has given us through revelation, HE then takes away the gift that was freely given. Which makes perfect sense. Let's understand what Paul is saying. First, GOD reveals the information, then HE gives us power. The reason HE gives us power is, so HIS information is more impacting than it is impressive. When we choose to change the information, then we lose the power. GOD is not going to allow HIS power to be impacting with the wrong information. Wrong information may be misleading, but it won't be impactful. People may be impressed with the wrong information, but they won't be empowered because GOD will remove the power.

- You can't bring down strongholds with the wrong information.
- You can't speak those things that are not as though they were with the wrong information.
- You can't speak to your mountains and make your mountains be cast into the sea with the wrong information.

Your words only receive power when you have the right information. That's why it's so important to be somewhere where you are receiving the right information. Remember what Paul said in verse 8 And I am the least of all the saints. So, if this type of power is working through me, individually, then imagine the type of power we can operate in collectively when the truth of GOD's Word is going forth.

Whenever the truth of GOD's Word is going forth, then the unlimited greatness of GOD's power is present. It's up to you, as a believer, to tap into that power. When we change the information, so we don't become offensive, then HIS power is not present and there's nothing to tap into. When there's nothing to tap into, then you become emotionally aroused rather than being spiritually empowered. Verse 10 lets us know the reason GOD wants us to be spiritually empowered, that, through The Church, GOD could let principalities in high places know HIS infinite wisdom.

Do you all see the assignments that have been given to The Church? Paul said, through The Church, GOD wants us to let principalities in high places know HIS infinite wisdom. Paul tells the Ephesians, that's why I'm praying for you to tap into the unlimited greatness of GOD's power. Look at what he tells the Ephesians in verses 14 through 16. Paul says, This is the reason I kneel in the presence of the Father from whom all the family in heaven and on earth receives its name. I'm asking GOD to give you a gift from the wealth of HIS glory. I pray that HE would give you inner strength and power through HIS SPIRIT.

Paul is not just talking about individually, he's talking about us as The Church collectively. This is the assignment of The Church. Not to come together and feel good, not to come together to be emotionally aroused, but to be able to speak to spiritual wickedness in high places. Until we start operating and tapping into the unlimited greatness of GOD's power, Paul says in verse 17 Then, CHRIST will live in you through Faith. I also pray that love may be the ground into which you sink your roots and on which you have your foundation.

So, let's put this together. Look at verses 16 and 17. Paul says, in order for CHRIST to live through us through Faith, we have to have inner strength and power through GOD's SPIRIT. The only way to have this inner strength and power is by tapping into it through the SPIRIT. In verse 17, once I tap into this unlimited greatness of GOD's power, which causes me to walk by Faith, instead of me walking around with arrogance, the foundation that I'm standing on is love. Basically, I don't have to change the information so I won't be offensive, because if my foundation is love, even though I'm telling the truth, it will be received in love. When your foundation is love, you can always stick to telling the truth.

Paul says in verses 18 and 19, This way, with all of GOD's people you will be able to understand how wide, long, high, and deep HIS love is. You will know CHRIST's love, which goes far beyond any knowledge. I am praying this so that you may be completely filled with GOD. I just love how the word of GOD interprets itself. Paul says when your foundation is love, you will then understand how deep GOD love is. Once you understand how GOD loves, you can tell people the truth about CHRIST, and they'll be able to receive it in love. Paul says in verse 19, You will know CHRIST's love, which goes far beyond any knowledge. Once you are completely filled with GOD, as Paul says in verse 19, when your foundation is love, you can tell someone the truth of GOD's Word, not to offend them, but because GOD loves them.

Every time I'm convicted by the truth of GOD's Word, that reminds me that GOD loves me. What that tells me is that GOD wants to get the glory out of me. GOD will never get the glory out of me if my lifestyle is opposite of the information that has been revealed to me. Once the information is no longer concealed, but has been revealed, instead of me being offended, that shows me that GOD loves me because HE only wants to get HIS glory out of me.

Paul says in verses 20 and 21, Glory belongs to GOD, whose power is at work in us. By this power, HE can do infinitely more than we can ask or imagine. Glory belongs to GOD in The Church and in CHRIST JESUS for all time and eternity! Amen. If glory belongs to GOD, HE should be able to get the glory from the power HE placed to work in us. Paul says in verse 20, By this power, HE can do more than we can ask or imagine. GOD will never get the glory if we don't tap into the power HE has provided for The Body to have. Are you tapping into this unlimited greatness of GOD's power?

Chapter 4
GOD's Gifts

CHRIST's Gifts to The Church
Verses 1-16

In chapter 3, Paul taught us the importance of us coming together as The Body. The more we come together, the more GOD is able to release HIS power through CHRIST's Body. When GOD's power is released through The Body, then GOD is able to get the glory. GOD gives us gifts so that when HE releases HIS power through the gift, HE will get the glory. That's why it's dangerous to take credit for something GOD has given your gift the power to do. When GOD operates HIS gift, GOD says I want people to see ME and not see you.

What a lot of people fail to realize is, in verse 7 Paul told us, the only way GOD's power was able to work through him was because the gift of the grace of GOD was given to him. After Paul was given the gift, he said then HIS power began to work through me. So, if GOD removes HIS power, then the gift becomes useless because HIS power is not present for your gift to tap into. When GOD's power is not present for you to tap into your gift, then you begin to say things that GOD didn't say.

Instead of prophesying, you end up prophe-lying. So, now you're giving people the wrong information to impress them; not the true word of GOD to impact and change their lives. When there's nothing to tap into, then you become emotionally aroused rather than being spiritually empowered. Your words only receive power when you have the right information.

Why does GOD give this type of power to The Church? Remember what Paul said in verse 10, HE did this so that now, through The Church (Body), we can let the rulers and authorities in high places know the infinite wisdom of GOD. GOD gives The Church the ability to be able to speak to spiritual wickedness and principalities, whenever the truth of GOD's Word is going forth. That's the assignment that has been given to us through The Church. The ability to be able to speak to demonic forces and to be effective when using our gifts. That's why Paul said in verse 16, ...I pray that HE would give you inner strength and power through HIS SPIRIT. Not so you can come together and feel good or be emotionally aroused. But, so you can be able to speak to spiritual wickedness in high places.

When we tap into this unlimited greatness of GOD's power, as Paul calls it, then GOD gets the glory. If glory belongs to GOD, HE should be able to get the glory from the power HE has placed in us to work through us. It's our job, as believers, The Church Body, to tap into the power that GOD has provided in us.

Chapter four is considered to be the beginning to the second half of the book of Ephesians. In the first half of Ephesians, Paul talked about the focus on GOD. The second half of the Ephesians will deal with the focus on you as a believer. Paul shifts his message from what GOD has done for you to what you can now do for GOD. The reason Paul's message shifts in this chapter is because even though GOD sees us for who we are, the world sees us for what we do.

What I mean by that is, GOD is only glorified through HIS people as we operate through the power of the HOLY SPIRIT. GOD is not glorified when we walk around in our understanding. GOD is only glorified when The Church imitates the characteristics of HIS SPIRIT. The characteristics Paul talks about in chapter four is humility, gentleness, patience, and the ability to love one another. If you can't love, walk in humility, gentleness, and patience, then you're not living up to the family name.

When Paul opens chapter four, he starts by talking about CHRIST's gift to The Church. Paul says, in verse 1, I, a prisoner in the Lord, en-courage you to live the kind of life which proves that GOD has called you. In chapter three he began the chapter by saying, "...I, Paul am the prisoner of Christ Jesus... Even being in prison, Paul says "I know I am in prison, as I write you this letter, but even being in prison, I'm not a prisoner of the system, but I am a prisoner of CHRIST."

When you are a prisoner of CHRIST, even though you may be under the world's system, you're not led by the system you're under. Paul says, "I'm being led by CHRIST." When you are led by CHRIST, you don't follow the system, even though you may be under it. The reason you're not led by the system is that you're not a prisoner of it. One thing for sure, you can't be a prisoner of CHRIST and also be led by the world's system.

That's why after Paul said he was a prisoner of CHRIST, I... encourage you to live the kind of life which proves that GOD has called you. The sad reality is a lot of believers follow the world's system more than they follow the ways of GOD. That's why Paul's message to the believers has always been to let the world be the world and let The Church be The Church. He is encouraging us to stop allowing the world to bring its ways into The Church. But, let The Church take its ways into the world.

We keep allowing the world to bring its ways into The Church. So now, the world has more influence over The Church than The Church influences the world. When the world has more influence over The Church, then The Church is identified with the world instead of The Church being identified with CHRIST. That's why it is easy for church folks to blend in with worldly folks and not be recognized, then it is for worldly folks to blend into The Church.

The life that Paul is talking about in 4:1 resembles the characteristics of GOD and not the ways of the world. What's the life that resembles GOD? I'm glad you asked. Look at verses 2 and 3, Be humble and gentle in every way. Be patient with each other and lovingly accept each other. Through the peace that ties you together, do your best to maintain the unity that the SPIRIT gives.

So, who gives it? The SPIRIT of GOD. If those are characteristics of GOD's SPIRIT, then those are characteristics of GOD. If GOD has placed HIS SPIRIT inside of me, and those are the characteristics of HIS SPIRIT, it shouldn't be difficult for me to operate in those characteristics. As believers, we shouldn't have a problem being humble, gentle, patient, and loving on another. Because one thing you can't be with GOD's SPIRIT is a "holy-hellion."

The reason it is impossible to be a "holy-hellion" is that Paul says in verse 4-6, There is one body and one SPIRIT, just as you were called in one hope of your calling; one Lord, one Faith, one baptism; one GOD and Father of all, who is above all, and through all, and in you all. You must either be "holy" or a "hellion." You can't be both. According to verse 6, if GOD is in you all, the only way you can be a hellion or resemble the world is by separating yourself from GOD. GOD can't be in you, but your lifestyle doesn't prove that you have been called by GOD. When GOD calls you, HE places HIS SPIRIT in you. That's why Paul said in chapter 3:7, HIS power began to work through me.

One of the evidence that GOD is with you is when there's evidence of HIS characteristics working through you. I can say GOD is in me all day long, but if there is no evidence of GOD's characteristics in me, then I'm just talking. Paul said in verse 4, There is one body and one SPIRIT. I can't be a part of The Body but be under the influence of another spirit. This One Body and One Spirit are in unity with each other.

Just like verse 5 and 6 says, There is one Lord, one Faith, one baptism, one God and Father of all, who is over everything, through everything, and in everything; with each other, so is the One Body and the One SPIRIT. Within this unity, Paul says GOD, who is above all, and through all, is in you all. The only way there can be no evidence of GOD characteristics is, I have to disconnect myself from this unity.

If GOD is in us all, we should be under the influence of one SPIRIT.

Remember what verse 4 just tells us, There is one body and one SPIRIT. That one SPIRIT operates the One Body. The only way there is division in The Church is, there has to be another spirit. GOD's SPIRIT is in unity with The One Body. If there is division by another spirit, then there must be another body. The other body is being controlled by another spirit because you can't have another spirit, a part of The Body that's in unity with GOD's SPIRIT.

Okay, let's bring it into the church. When you see someone bringing worldly ways into the church, they are being controlled by a worldly spirit. I don't care how they try to be a part of The Body by coming into the church. If they are being controlled by a worldly spirit, then they are a part of another body and not The Body of CHRIST. The Body of CHRIST is the One Body that's under the influence of one spirit, one Lord, one Faith, one baptism; one GOD and Father.

Anytime you find someone who has a problem with being attached to the One Body that's controlled by the One SPIRIT, it's because they haven't been called by GOD to be attached to the One Body. Anyone who's been called by GOD doesn't have a problem being attached to the One Body because they are in unity with the same One SPIRIT. Just because someone is in the same building doesn't mean they represent the One Body. That's why Paul tells us in verse 1, ...to live the kind of life which proves that you have been called by GOD.

If someone's life isn't producing the evidence that GOD has called them, they may not be a part of The One Body that Paul talks about in verse 4. You can't be a part of this One Body that's influenced by One SPIRIT and not produce the evidence of GOD's SPIRIT. If the evidence that someone is producing is the opposite of GOD's SPIRIT, then they have shown evidence of not producing what GOD's SPIRIT's characteristics are. Here are a few more examples:

GOD's SPIRIT is humble. The opposite of humility is arrogance.

GOD's SPIRIT is gentleness. The opposite of gentleness is unkind.

GOD's SPIRIT is patience. The opposite of patience is impatience.

GOD's SPIRIT is love. The opposite of love is hatred.

If someone is producing arrogance, meanness, impatience, hatred, and confusion, even though they're in the same building, they are not a part of The One Body. We think, just because they are in the same building, that makes them a part of The One Body. The sad reality is, those who are under the other spirit, the worldly spirit, identifies The Church Body more than GOD's SPIRIT does. And that's a problem! The Church should never be labeled as messy, arrogant, mean, and unloving because those are not the characteristics of GOD.

If I am a follower of CHRIST, which makes me a part of The Body, then I should be identified by the one SPIRIT that influences The Body. If I am a believer, I should be identified by being humble and not arrogant. If I am a part of The One Body, I should be identified by being loving and not hateful. I should be identified by being caring and not unconcerned.

After Paul talks about The Church being One Body and One Spirit, he then talks about spiritual gifts. And for some reason, a lot of people think spiritual gifts separate them from The Body. As they see the results of GOD's power, they begin to take ownership of the gift that belongs to GOD. You can't operate a spiritual gift being separated from The Body. When you separate from The Body, then you are operating under another spirit. GOD is not glorified when we operate under another spirit. GOD is only glorified when The Church imitates the characteristics of GOD's SPIRIT.

People experience GOD when we live according to the characteristics of HIS SPIRIT. I think that's only fair. If GOD allows me to have HIS SPIRIT, when people come in contact with me, they should come in contact with HIM. When they can see a change in me, it helps to create a change in them. If GOD has placed HIS SPIRIT inside of me, it shouldn't be difficult for me to operate in those characteristics. If humility, gentleness, patience, and the ability to love are characteristics of GOD's SPIRIT, then those are characteristics of GOD.

As a believer, it shouldn't be a problem being humble, gentle, kind, patient, and loving. The only way it would be a problem is that you don't have GOD's SPIRIT. The only way someone will not be able to produce the characteristics of GOD's SPIRIT is, HIS SPIRIT does not live in them. I can't be a part of The One Body but be under the influence of another spirit.

This One Body is in unity with The One SPIRIT. You can't have another spirit being attached to The One Body and still be in unity with GOD's SPIRIT. Anytime you find someone who has a problem with being attached to The One Body, it's because they are under the influence of another spirit.

Why? Verse 4 just told us The One Body is in unity with the one SPIRIT. When someone never gets along with The Body, it's because they are a part of another spirit. The only way we can prove that we have been called by GOD is by producing the evidence of GOD's SPIRIT. Galatians 5:25 says, If we live by our spiritual nature, then our lives need to conform to our spiritual nature.

Galatians 5:19-21 also tells us the characteristics of the other spirit; perversion, sexually unclean, idolatry, sorcery, hatred, rivalry, jealousy, angry outbursts, selfish ambition, conflict, rebellion, heresies, envy, drunkenness, participating in sinful activities. Paul, also being the author of Galatians, tells us not only are these considered characteristics of the corrupt nature but also that you can't even get into the Kingdom of GOD being identified with and practicing these characteristics.

After Paul tells us there is only One Body influenced by the same One SPIRIT, he then proves his point in verse 7 by telling us GOD's favor has been given to each of us. It was measured out to us by CHRIST who gave it. GOD's favor and grace were given to every one a part of The One Body. There is never a reason for you to be identified by another spirit. Why? It was measured and given to us by CHRIST. The only way you can be identified by another spirit is by not being a part of The One Body. Everyone who is a part of CHRIST's Body can be identified by GOD's favor because CHRIST gave it to us.

Paul says in verses 8-10, That's why the Scriptures say: "When HE went to the highest place, HE took captive those who had captured us and gave gifts to people." Now what does it mean that HE went up except that HE also had gone down to the lowest parts of the earth? The one who had gone down also went up above all the heavens so that HE fills everything. To say that you can still be a part of The One Body and not by the same One SPIRIT is to say that CHRIST did not have enough power to set the captives free. In other words, if you are a part of the same One Body, influenced by the same One SPIRIT, The One Body only operates according to the powers of the One SPIRIT.

When CHRIST set the captives free, HE distributed the characteristics of GOD's SPIRIT into The One Body. When people see The One Body, it is identified by the same One SPIRIT. If someone is identified by another spirit, that means they are not a part of the same One Body. When CHRIST distributed GOD's characteristics in The Body, HE also distributed GOD's gifts to The Body. Not only are we identified by GOD's characteristics, but we're also identified by GOD's gifts that are also controlled by GOD's One SPIRIT.

Look at what Paul says in verse 11, HE also gave apostles, prophets, missionaries, as well as pastors and teachers as gifts to HIS church. For some reason, a lot of people think spiritual gifts separate them from The Body. You can't operate GOD's spiritual gifts being separated from The Body. Anytime you separate from The Body, you are operating under another spirit.

GOD is not going to allow HIS SPIRIT to operate outside of The Body of CHRIST. That's why Paul said in verses 4-6, There is one body and one SPIRIT. Just as you were called in one hope of your calling; one Lord, one Faith, one baptism; one GOD and Father of all, who is above all, and through all, lives in you all.

So basically, there are no solo acts in the Kingdom of GOD. The only One who can operate solo is CHRIST. According to Paul in verse 5, even CHRIST is in unity with the same One SPIRIT because there is only one Lord. You can separate yourself from The Body if you want to. But if you do, you won't be operating under the power of the same One SPIRIT because GOD won't be in you. You can only tap into GOD's power when you are attached to The One Body of CHRIST. When you detach from The One Body, then you must tap into another spirit. And that spirit is witchcraft.

Here's the reason why it takes GOD's SPIRIT to operate HIS gifts and why you can't tap into HIS SPIRIT being disconnected from The Body. Verse 12 reads, Their purpose is to prepare GOD's people, to serve, and to build up The Body of CHRIST. If the purpose of GOD's gift is to build up The Body of CHRIST, then why would GOD give someone the power to operate HIS gift if it is not going to build up The Body of CHRIST? The reason GOD gives gifts to The Body of CHRIST is to prepare GOD's people, to serve, and to build up The Body of CHRIST, right? So, GOD gives gifts to benefit The Body of CHRIST.

Some have separated themselves from The Body of CHRIST by charging believers a monetary fee. Yes, a fee. If the only way I use my gift is by charging you a monetary fee, then how is that building up The Body of CHRIST? If I put a charge on the gift GOD gave me to prepare HIS people, to serve, and to build up The Body of CHRIST, how is that benefiting The Body of CHRIST?

If I'm attached to The Body, how can I charge The Body

that I am attached to for using my gift? That's just like my legs telling my arms, "I'll take you where you need to go for a $250 seed offering." My gift should benefit The Body and not me. If I'm the only one benefiting from my gift, then I have detached myself from The Body.

Watch this, even if my legs ask my arms for a $250 seed offering. Because my arms and legs are attached to the same One Body, then the seed offering should benefit the whole Body. The only way it will only benefit the legs is, the legs have to detach themselves from The Body. Anything that detaches itself from The Body is controlled by another spirit.

All of GOD's gifts prepare GOD's people to serve and to build up The One Body of CHRIST because CHRIST doesn't have another body. That's why Paul says in verse 5, There is one Lord and one Faith. So, there can only be one CHRIST Body that's in unity with the same one Lord who is in unity with the same One SPIRIT. Anyone who steps outside of The One Body is influenced by another spirit.

Now, the Bible does say in Proverbs 18:16, your gift will make room for you. But your gift is only going to make room for you, so you can benefit The Body. When GOD blesses The Body through our gifts, then we become recipients of the blessing. Everything that's attached to The Body benefits from everything heaven has to offer to The Body.

Look what Paul says in the next couple of verses, 13-14, This is to continue until all of us are united in our Faith and in our knowledge about GOD's Son until we become mature until we measure up to CHRIST, who is the standard. Then we will no longer be little children, tossed and carried about by all kinds of teachings that change like the wind. We will no longer be influenced by people who use cunning and clever strategies to lead us astray. That was so powerful!

People who are easily detached from The Body are people who are not mature in their Faith. Paul says at some point you have to become mature in your Faith. At some point clichés and catchy phrases shouldn't keep exciting you. At some point, you should hunger for the truth of GOD's Word and not just believe what anybody tells you. If it can't be backed up with Scripture, then I don't receive it. You have to get off of spiritual junk food and start feasting on the truth of GOD's Word to the point where anything else is wasting your time. Faith comes by hearing and hearing by the word of GOD. (Romans 10:17) If you're not going to increase my Faith in the Word of GOD, then you have wasted time.

When you are a babe in CHRIST, baby food is okay. There is nothing wrong with being a baby Christian when you first get saved. As a matter of fact, it's kind of cute! But who wants to keep feeding and changing diapers on a grown person? It's not cute anymore. It becomes pretty pathetic when you have to keep treating grown folks like children.

Paul said the reason you keep being detached from The Body is that you are being influenced by other people who keep leading you astray. Paul said at some point it's time to grow up! If every time you hear a rumor, you leave, Paul says grow up! If every time something in The Body doesn't go your way causes you to detach yourself from The Body, Paul says grow up! Verses 15 and 16 say, Instead, as we lovingly speak the truth, we will grow up completely in our relationship to CHRIST, who is the Head. HE makes the whole Body fit together and unites it through the support of every joint. As each and every part does its job, HE makes The Body grow so that it builds itself up in love.

It's the truth of GOD's Word that causes you to grow up spiritually.
It's the truth of GOD's Word that causes you to increase your Faith.
It's the truth of GOD's Word that causes us to become closer to GOD.
It's the truth of GOD's Word that makes us more effective in the Body.

If I can only experience spiritual growth from the truth of GOD's

Word, but I'm not growing, then that means I'm rejecting the truth of GOD's Word, because I would rather be on spiritual junk food. Just because someone prepares a healthy meal doesn't mean everyone chooses to eat it. Some people like spiritual junk food. Just like junk food is unhealthy for the body, spiritual junk is not healthy for your spirit.

Paul just told us in verse 14, spiritual junk food causes you not to grow. Not growing causes you to be disconnected from The Body. That's why Paul says what he says in verse 17, So, I tell you and encourage you in the Lord's name not to live any longer like other people in the world. Their minds are set on worthless things.

Chapter 5

GOD's Characteristics

Imitate GOD
Verses 1-20

In chapter 5, Paul continues to deal with behavior in The Body of CHRIST. Paul's message, in this chapter, is how The Church is supposed to imitate GOD. When the world comes into contact with The Church Body, they're supposed to experience GOD. Not only experience the characteristics of GOD, but the gifts of GOD. What we do represents the GOD we serve.

When I want to give in to some of my fleshly desires, if what I want is going to bring shame to The Body, I should be willing to beat my flesh into submission and tell my flesh no. Tell your flesh:

- You can't say that flesh.
- You have to be obedient, flesh.
- Hold your tongue, flesh.
- I know they deserve to be cussed out, but somebody is watching you, flesh.

Why would I allow the person I used to be, ruin everything that GOD has changed? Not only would it ruin me, but it will also bring shame to The Body.

Paul uses the technique of comparing opposites to illustrate the difference between godly and ungodly living. For example, he compares light to darkness, wisdom to foolishness, and GOD's power to the power of darkness. We know that there is no comparison between the kingdom of darkness and The Kingdom of God. But, the message Paul is trying to give us is, if we don't embrace the light, then darkness will consume us. If old things have passed away and behold all things have become new, it shouldn't be difficult for me to walk in the characteristics of GOD. (2 Corinthians 5:17) When you imitate GOD, you can't be consumed by darkness. Why? Because there is no darkness in GOD. If we don't embrace GOD's power, then the power of darkness will overtake us. We can't live in between two opposites, especially, when you are a follower of CHRIST.

The moment you become a follower of CHRIST, even when you embrace GOD's power, darkness will still chase you. Could you imagine what would happen if you don't embrace GOD's power? You will eventually be overtaken by the powers of darkness. This is why it's so easy for people to tap into darkness whenever they detached themselves from The Body.

When GOD removes HIS power from them, and they operate HIS gift HE gave them, they have to tap into another power. Most people tap into darkness whenever GOD's Spirit is not present. For example, whenever a prophet of GOD detached himself from The Body, since GOD is no longer speaking to him through HIS SPIRIT, he has to tap into darkness to get information.

Paul's message in this chapter is for us to imitate GOD. In verse 1, Paul tells the believers, Therefore be imitators of GOD as dear children. Now, notice what Paul says in verse 1. He doesn't just tell us to imitate GOD, but he tells us to imitate GOD as HIS children. For any parent who raised children, whether those children turned out to be good or bad, you will always see some of your characteristics in that child. Of course, we want them to carry on our positive characteristics and traits. However, that's not always the case. That's why there are some things you should not do in front of your children. You never know what traits they're going to pick up. Some traits, whether good or bad, have more influence over children.

Paul says it's okay to imitate GOD as one of HIS children, because all of HIS traits are good. You can't pick up any bad traits when you are imitating

GOD. Every area in our lives we choose to imitate GOD will be victorious. There's nothing about GOD that can be defeated. I can never say I did it GOD's way, and came out of it a failure. Why? GOD doesn't fail.

Most times, our fleshly desires try to convince us that it is GOD. Anytime your fleshly desire tries to convince you it's GOD's desire, your flesh has to try to convince you that the decision you're making is right. If you have to convince yourself that something is right, it's probably wrong. I don't have to convince myself to love my neighbor or that sex was ordained for marriage. For example, "Man, this feels so right, so it must be GOD." Well, if it is GOD, don't defile the bedroom by having sex before marriage.

Paul says to imitate GOD as a child would imitate their parents. When you imitate GOD, there's nothing bad about GOD to imitate. I can never be wrong or fall short by imitating GOD. I only fall short and am wrong when I follow my flesh and try to justify my desires as something GOD wants.

When we run the DNA of all of our mistakes, we will realize that our flesh fathered that decision instead of GOD. What does the Bible say? The blessings of the Lord make us rich and add no sorrow. (Proverbs 10:22) It's never GOD's intent for us to produce sorrow. We only produce sorrow when we walk in the flesh. To prove that, verse 2 says Live in love as CHRIST also loved us. HE gave HIS life for us as an offering and sacrifice, a soothing aroma to GOD.

Paul said when CHRIST imitated GOD, it was a sweet smell in the nostrils of GOD. CHRIST imitated GOD by walking in love. Love is a characteristic of GOD. How did CHRIST walk in love? HE walked in love by giving HIS life for us as an offering and a sacrifice. Love caused HIM to give HIS life for us. When CHRIST imitated GOD's love, it was a sweet aroma to the nostrils of GOD. When something has a sweet aroma, it makes you bask in its ambiance.

Let's put verses 1 and 2 into perspective. Whenever we imitate the characteristics of GOD, GOD savors in the moment. Could you imagine being the cause of GOD savoring a moment? To savor in something means to enjoy or to find pleasure in. When we imitate GOD by walking in the characteristics of GOD, not only is it pleasing to GOD, but HE also finds pleasure in that moment.

If GOD is finding pleasure in a moment that we created, HE's not going to allow the enemy to come and take HIS moment of pleasure away. Now, the flip side to that is, when we walk in the flesh, we allow our flesh to take that moment of pleasure away from GOD. Fleshly moments don't bring a sweet aroma to GOD, but it stinks in the nostrils of GOD; regardless of how right it feels to our flesh. Every situation we find ourselves in, we should ask ourselves the question, "Is GOD finding pleasure in this situation?" That's why Paul told us it grieves the HOLY SPIRIT when our falling short turns into a practice. It's our job, as The Body, to catch each other in our falling short before it becomes a practice.

Verses 3-5, Don't let sexual sin, perversion of any kind, or greed even be mentioned among you. This is not appropriate behavior for GOD's holy people. It's not right that dirty stories, foolish talk, or obscene jokes should be mentioned among you either. Instead, give thanks to GOD. You know very well that no person who is involved in sexual sin, perversion, or greed (which means worshiping wealth) can have any inheritance in the kingdom of CHRIST and of GOD.

According to verse 5, anything that displeases GOD can't enter into the kingdom of GOD; funk can't enter into heaven. For those who are teaching that heaven is going to be full of sinners, I'm glad Paul says what he says next in verse 6. Let no one deceive you with empty words, for because of these things, the wrath of GOD comes upon the sons of disobedience. For those who try to make people feel comfortable about living in their sins, just to keep their church full, they're not helping them, they're destroying them. Paul says these things cause the wrath of GOD to come upon them. As a matter of fact, in verse 7, Paul says, Don't even be partners with them. In other words, don't support their foolishness.

All sin stinks in the nostrils of GOD. If sin stinks in the nostrils of GOD, when we commit them down here, how is HE going to allow that bad smell to enter into heaven? Verse 3 Paul says, this is not appropriate behavior. The New King James Version says, let it not even be named among you. In other words, it's a danger to be identified by the sins you are practicing.

No one should be able to look at you and identify you according to your sins. Why? Verse 8 says, Once you lived in the dark, but now the Lord has filled you with light. Live as children who have light. If I am identified by the sins that I am practicing, instead of it showing GOD's light, it shows the world the darkness that I once lived in. How can my life represent light when my lifestyle represents darkness? Paul is making a point to say, it's not okay to be known by your sinful behavior; this is not appropriate behavior.

In verses 9 and 10, Paul tells us the reason we should live by GOD's light, Light produces everything that is good, that has GOD's approval, and that is true. Determine which things please the Lord. According to Paul, we have a choice; walk in GOD's light or walk in darkness, live by the SPIRIT or live according to our flesh. Paul says it's not rocket science. When we choose to live by GOD's light, Light produces everything that is good.

Why would I want to produce anything other than good by following my flesh? Our flesh will get us in trouble every time. Since living by light or darkness, by the Spirit or by the flesh is a choice, and living by the Spirit produces that which is good and living according to the flesh produces problems. I can't get mad at GOD when it was my choice in what I produced. If you want confusion and chaos, follow the flesh. If you want to produce everything good, Paul says, imitate GOD.

Verse 11 tells us to Have nothing to do with the useless works that darkness produces. Instead, expose them for what they are. After Paul tells us not to have anything to do with darkness, he reminds us that we are responsible for helping our brother or sister who are living in darkness. Whose falling short is about to turn into a practice. When they look bad, they make The Body look bad. When they are identified by sin, it makes The Body be identified with the sin they are practicing. I don't know about you, but I don't want to be identified by anyone else's sin. Especially, sins they choose to practice, since Paul tells us it's a choice in verse 10.

We should never be quick to describe our practices as falling short. When you fall short, it's easy to continue in well-doing. When you are practicing sin, you are continually falling short. As I stated earlier, Paul is telling the Ephesians that your falling short should never turn into a practice. That's why he says in verse 8, Live as children who have light and have nothing to do with darkness.

What we don't realize about darkness is that it is like cancer that produces things we are not ready to deal with. Look at verse 11 again, Have nothing to do with the useless works that darkness produces. My question is, if light and darkness is a choice that we choose, then why would anyone choose darkness over light? Especially, being a follower of CHRIST.

Well, the answer is found in verses 12-14, It is shameful to talk about what some people do in secret. Light exposes the true character of everything because light makes everything easy to see. That's why it says: "Wake up, sleeper! Rise from the dead, and CHRIST will shine on you. We're not supposed to hide darkness, but we're supposed to expose it with the truth.

Then after Paul tells us to expose darkness by living in the light, he then gives us instructions followed by a warning in verses 15-20, So then, be very careful how you live. Don't live like foolish people but like wise people. Make the most of your opportunities because these are evil days. So don't be foolish, but understand what the Lord wants. Don't get drunk on wine, which leads to wild living. Instead, be filled with the Spirit by reciting psalms, hymns, and spiritual songs for your own good. Sing and make music to the Lord with your hearts. Always thank GOD the Father for everything in the name of our Lord JESUS CHRIST.

What's going to help me to walk in the SPIRIT? Paul said by being filled with the SPIRIT. By reciting psalms, hymns, and spiritual songs for your own good. Sing and make music to the Lord with your hearts. By always giving thanks, GOD.

Watch how clever Paul was. In verse 18, he uses being drunk with wine in comparison to being filled with the HOLY SPIRIT. Not that something is wrong with drinking wine, but when you are filled with wine, to the point of drunkenness, it causes a certain outcome. That outcome can cause you to sin. When you are filled with the HOLY SPIRIT, it causes a certain type of drunkenness, but the outcome is not sin. Being drunk with wine causes you to sin, being drunk with the HOLY SPIRIT causes you to live right.

The reason Paul compared the HOLY SPIRIT to drinking wine is because whenever a person gets drunk, it's obvious that they are under the influence of alcohol. Paul is telling us, just like it's obvious that someone is under the influence of alcohol, it should be just as obvious when someone is under the influence of the HOLY SPIRIT. Just like there are aftereffects of being intoxicated with alcohol, which is a hangover, there are also aftereffects of being intoxicated by the HOLY SPIRIT, which are the Fruits of the Spirit. When someone is intoxicated from alcohol, because of the influence of the alcohol, you never know what they may do or say.

When someone is intoxicated from the HOLY SPIRIT, because the aftereffects are the Fruits of the Spirit, when the enemy despitefully uses you, he thinks you're going to respond in hatred. But, because you are under the influence of the HOLY SPIRIT you respond in love. Paul says, allow the HOLY SPIRIT to influence you the same way you would allow alcohol to influence you if you were intoxicated. The hangover from the HOLY SPIRIT causes you to imitate the characteristics of GOD, which then changes your outcome. What did verse 9 tell us the outcome is? Light always produces everything that is good. Alcohol produces sin and vomit.

The HOLY SPIRIT produces everything good!

Unity & Not Authority
Verses 21-33

Then after Paul warns us by giving us instructions, he then makes, what seems to be, the most controversial statement in the whole Bible by using the "S" word. And no, it's not the word stupid; it's submit. Most people think this word submit is a bad word. Because they don't understand Paul's definition, they have a hard time doing it. What does submission mean to you?

When someone is trying to control someone else, they are quick to recite verse 22, Wives, submit to your own husbands, as to the Lord. (KJV) I consider verse 21 as one of the most hidden verses in the Bible, where Paul tells us to submit to one another in the fear of GOD. (KJV) Everyone is quick to recite verse 22, but no one wants to recite verse 21. You can't embrace verse 22 without first applying verse 21. If you only recite verse 22 without verse 21, then you make the whole text an oxymoron.

Whenever you are reading Scripture, it must always be taken in context. When I say taken in context, all that simply means is, that which goes with the text. Context helps give meaning to the text you are reading. If you fail to add the text that goes with the text you are reading, then you have taken that text out of context.

You can't understand verse 22 without understanding verse 21; verse 21 gives meaning to verse 22. One thing for sure is, Paul does not go from talking about being in unity as a Body, to talking about us being in authority to someone else. Let's understand what Paul is telling us when he tells us to submit, and how all this falls in line with what Paul has already been teaching us about unity as One Body.

Paul has already been teaching us that every believer is a part of The Body. The only one who is the Head of The Body is CHRIST. If Paul is telling us to submit and CHRIST is already the Head, by me submitting to you does not put you in authority over me. What does Paul say in verse 21? Submit to one another in the fear of GOD.

So, if Paul has been teaching us about unity, then the rest of the verses that talk about submitting are not talking about authority. It's talking about unity as well. When we learn how to submit one to the other, then The Body will work together in unity. Unity creates harmony. When we don't submit to each other, it causes confusion in The Body. Submitting to someone is not about if they asked you to jump, you say how hi. Love should make you do that.

I like how Paul uses the word submit in verse 21 and then uses the same word to talk about wives submitting to your husbands in verse 22. Verse 21's submit can't be talking about getting along with each other, and then in verse 22's submit is talking about authority. The same submit in verse 21 is the same submit in verse 22. So, let's get a clear understanding of this word that Paul uses in verses 21 and 22. When Paul uses the word submit, Paul is talking about the function and the order within a union and not control and authority.

So, with that being said, the submission that wives are to show to their husbands in verse 22, is an example of the submission that we all are supposed to show each other in verse 21. This submission that's supposed to be between all believers and wives to their husbands is supposed to represent order and not authority.

The first thing to note, when keeping everything in context is, what Paul is NOT doing is taking a break from talking about unity and imitating CHRIST, in order to deal with marriage. When you go down to verse 32, Paul is saying the reason he's even mentioning husband and wives is because This is a great mystery, but I speak concerning CHRIST and The

Church. So basically, the relationship between CHRIST and The Church should be the same relationship between husband and wife.

When you put that into context, CHRIST being the Husband and The Church being HIS wife, Paul is not trying to set husbands straight and put wives in their place. He's trying to show us the relationship CHRIST has with The Church, and that relationship is like a marriage between husband and wife. Now, keeping that concept in mind that CHRIST is the Husband and The Church Body is the wife, look at what verses 22-25 says, Wives, submit to your own husbands, as to the Lord. For the husband is head of the wife, as also CHRIST is Head of the church; and HE is the Savior of the Body. Therefore, just as the church is subject to CHRIST, so let the wives be to their own husbands in everything. Husbands, love your wives, just as CHRIST also loved the church and gave Himself for her.

If CHRIST is the Husband and The Church Body is the wife, it's evident that CHRIST loves us because HE gave HIS life for us. Because CHRIST loves us, we as The Church Body are supposed to submit under CHRIST. It's easy for The Church to submit under CHRIST because we know HE loves us because HE was willing to give HIS life for us.

Even though Paul is using the relationship between a husband and wife to describe the relationship between CHRIST and The Church, should we pattern our marriages after this description? Most definitely! If husbands don't love their wives like CHRIST loves The Church, then he is out of order. If a man can't see himself loving someone like CHRIST loves The Church, then HE shouldn't make her HIS wife. The relationship between husband and wife should resemble, or should I say imitate the relationship between CHRIST and The Church.

Now, that's the love part. Let's deal with the submit part. Paul says, The Church is supposed to submit to CHRIST the same way as a wife submits to her husband. To make sure we keep verse 22 in context, let's understand verse 21. Before Paul says wife submit to your husband, he first says in verse 21 submitting yourselves one to the other in the fear of GOD.

So, submitting ourselves one to the other as a Body should resemble the same way wives submit themselves to their husbands. Now, let's understand the connection. When Paul says wives submit to your husbands, what Paul is saying is, in a marriage, there is the role of the husband and there's also the role of the wife. When we submit to each other, all we're doing is, allowing the other person to play the role that they have been designed for without us interfering with them playing their role.

If we are The Church Body, somebody's role is the hand, somebody else's role is the arm, another's role is the feet, somebody's role is the leg, and so on! How the leg submits to the arm is by allowing the arm to be the arm and not trying to take the place of the arm. How the pastor submits to the doorkeepers is by allowing the doorkeepers to be doorkeepers. How we submit one to the other is by allowing each other to operate in the role that GOD called one another to, without us trying to play their role that GOD didn't call us to.

So, wives, let your husband play the role of the husband and husbands, allow your wife to play the role of the wife. When we allow each other to play their role, then we are submitting one to the other, which then creates unity for The Body to operate accordingly. When everyone plays their role, we have unity instead of division, and peace instead of confusion.

Here's why it's important for everybody in The Body to play their own role. Verses 26 and 27 tells us that HE might sanctify and cleanse her with the washing of water by the word, that HE might present her to Himself a glorious church, not having spot or wrinkle or any such thing, but that she should be holy and without blemish. When CHRIST loves The Church and The Church submits under CHRIST by following CHRIST, HE's able to present us before GOD without spot or wrinkle.

When all a couple can do is find spots and wrinkles in each other, then the problem could be they're not allowing the other one to play their role.

Or the problem could be, the husband doesn't love his wife like CHRIST loves The Church, which makes it hard for her to submit. Paul reiterates verse 25 in verses 28 and 29 by saying, So husbands ought to love their own wives as their own bodies; he who loves his wife loves himself. For no one ever hated his own flesh but nourishes and cherishes it, just as the Lord does the church.

When husbands don't love their wives like CHRIST loves The Church, then mistreatment and abuse take place. If he loves his wife like CHRIST loves The Church, then he wouldn't cheat on his wife because CHRIST never cheated on The Church. So, once again, when Paul uses this word submit, he's talking about unity and not authority.

What does Paul say in verse 29? For no one ever hated his own flesh but nourishes and cherishes it, just as the LORD does The Church. So, because CHRIST operated in the characteristics of love, not only did HE nourish it and cherish it, but HE also died for it. Just like a husband and a wife become one flesh, look at what Paul says in verse 30, For we are members of HIS Body, of HIS flesh and of HIS bones.

Please understand that Paul is using the relationship between a husband and a wife to describe the relationship between CHRIST and The Church. The relationship that Paul uses between a husband and a wife is a relationship that has been ordained by GOD. He's not talking about a marriage that just got together, but he's talking about a marriage that GOD put together. When you look at all the examples that Paul is using regarding the marriage between husband and wife and CHRIST and The Church, he's talking about a relationship that's acceptable to GOD.

Paul said, when CHRIST presents HIS bride to GOD, she has to be without spot or wrinkle, holy without blemish. CHRIST is not trying to present a Church Body to GOD that's always fussing and fighting that can't submit itself to one another, and definitely, that doesn't love each other.

In verse 32 Paul says, This is a great mystery, but I speak concerning

CHRIST and The Church. The example he is referring to between CHRIST and The Church is the union that has been ordained by GOD. What GOD has joined together; no man can come in between. (Paraphrased Mark 10:9)

Then he closes out chapter 5 with verse 33 by saying, Nevertheless let each one of you in particular so love his own wife as himself, and let the wife see that she respects her husband. Just as a marriage should have unity in its union, so does The Body of Christ. If we are a part of The Body, we should love each other the same way a husband loves his wife. If we are a part of the Body of Christ, we are supposed to respect each other the same way a wife respects her husband.

The relationship between husband and wife is not one of authority, but it is a relationship of unity. The relationship between those who are a part of The Body of CHRIST is not one of authority, but it should be the same relationship between a husband and his wife; a relationship of unity!

Chapter 6

GOD's Armor

Now, before we dive into chapter 6, I think it would be wise for us to make sure we understand everything Paul taught the Ephesians, so we can understand how chapter 6 relates to his teachings. If we don't understand Paul's main message to the Ephesians, we'll take chapter 6 out of context. In chapter 6, Paul deals with things that are very controversial. People, to this day, still disagree with some of the things that are written in chapter 6. Notice, I said written in chapter 6, instead of what Paul taught in chapter 6. Especially the advice Paul gives regarding slaves and masters.

A lot of people like to say man just interjected verses 5 through 9 into Ephesians to control slaves. What people forget is, Paul is talking to The Body of CHRIST, the believers, who have confessed JESUS as Lord and not to society. If a slave wanted to accept CHRIST, that meant that he was now a believer of CHRIST, but to society, he was still a slave. The book of Galatians teaches us, as believers, that even though you can be oppressed by society, you can still have freedom in CHRIST.

Paul was never trying to change society, but he was trying to change the mindset of the believer. When you can change the mindset of the believer, when society decides to become a believer. They are now under the same mindset; believer's mindset. When you are under the mindset of the believer, then your behavior should act according to the mindset of someone who believes. I can't be a follower of CHRIST who gives me freedom, and keep you, a believer, in bondage.

If you are a believer and I am a believer, that means we are a part of the same One Body. Remember what Paul told us in Ephesians chapter 4 verses 4-6. There is One Body and One Spirit, just as you were called in one hope of your calling; one Lord, one Faith, one baptism; one GOD and Father of all, who is above all, and through all, and in you all. If we are a part of the same One Body that's controlled by the same One Spirit and the same GOD is the Father of us all, how can I keep you in bondage? I can't. If The Body is divided, then how are we going to fight spiritual warfare as a Body? We can't fight spiritual warfare separated.

What is the purpose of The Body? Well, the first thing, The Body is the expression of the Head. It's supposed to express and perform the desires of the Head. Remember what I discussed in the introduction of this book, if my hand rubs my head, it's not because my hand had a desire to rub my head, my hands only did what the head told it to do. The only time The Body does not execute the commands of the Head is when it's involuntary.

For example, if you hit a certain part of my knee, it will automatically cause my leg to jump involuntarily; involuntary reflex. The head didn't tell my leg to move, something hit it and caused it to move. Spiritually, we can call that spiritual wickedness. That's why Paul teaches us in chapter 6, to put on the whole Armor of GOD, so spiritual wickedness won't cause The Body to act out involuntarily. The Armor of GOD protects The Body from anything hitting it to cause it to respond involuntarily.

When people don't have on the whole Armor of GOD, and spiritual wickedness hits them, it causes them to respond involuntarily. Paul has been telling us that as believers we're supposed to imitate GOD. When we imitate GOD, it causes us, as a Body, not to respond involuntarily. That's why Paul told us in chapter 5:11 that we should Have nothing to do with darkness because darkness produces everything that is not of GOD. It's important that we walk in the Fruits of the Spirit. Anything our flesh produces, produces darkness. But, everything the Spirit produces, Paul said it is good.

When the Spirit produces everything good, everything is in harmony, unity, and on one accord. When we are on one accord as One Body and One Spirit, one hope; one Lord, one Faith, one baptism; one GOD and Father, then The Body is effective when battling spiritual wickedness. It is safe to say that the main focus of Paul's message in the book of Ephesians has been The Church operating as One Body in unity. To have unity in The Body, there has to be order, not authority, but order.

Advice to Children & Parent
Verses 1-4

When we enter into chapter 6, Paul closes his letter to the Ephesians with a list of instructions regarding spiritual warfare. The book of Ephesians is important to us as believers because if we are not on one accord as One Body, Paul knew the devil has multiple strategies and tricks which he doesn't hesitate to use towards society. Watch this, but only The Church has the ability to stop him. The Church is spiritually equipped to fight spiritual warfare.

Now, notice I said the devil won't hesitate to use his powers towards society. The devil doesn't have any power over The Church. JESUS tells us in Matthew 16:18 ...and upon this rock I will build my Church and the gates of hell shall not prevail against it. The Church is controlled by GOD. It's the devil's job to make The Church think we don't have power that we already have. If The Church is not operating in GOD's power and authority, then there's no one to fight the devil. There's no one to fight spiritual wickedness in high places because we're too busy fighting each other.

That's why there must be unity in The Body. When there's unity in The Body, The Body can effectively operate in GOD's authority. Just like there's a balance that causes unity in The Church, there is also a balance that causes unity between husbands and wives. Just like there is a balance that causes unity between husbands and wives, there's also a balance that causes unity between parents and their children.

That's why Paul opens up chapter 6 by telling children in verse 1 ...to obey their parents... Because not only does Paul tells children to obey their parents in verse 1, but he also continues to tell children in verses 2 and

3 to Honor your father and mother, which is the first commandment with promise. Here's why, that it may be well with you and you may live long on the earth.

Not only are kids to obey their parents, but Paul said they're supposed to also honor them. Obeying and honoring are two different things. Honor goes beyond obedience. As a parent, I'm supposed to make sure I give my children something to honor. It's easy for kids to obey you when you give them something to honor. The blessing that comes to them from obeying and honoring their parents, Paul said, will cause them to live long on the earth.

I'm glad Paul says what he says in verse 4, And you, fathers, do not provoke your children to wrath, but bring them up in the training and admonition of the Lord. When parents provoke their kids, it's hard for them to honor and obey their parents. Now, provoking your kids doesn't give them the right not to honor and obey their parents, but provoking them makes it harder for them to honor and obey their parents.

Could you imagine as a parent provoking your children to the point whereby, they no longer want to honor and obey you, and then it causes them not to live a long life on the earth? That's one guilt I wouldn't want to feel. If something were to happen to my children, and then I have to realize I was a bad parent. If the charge to the parents in verse 4 is not to provoke their children to anger, then, "do as I say and not as I do" doesn't apply to being a parent.

I have to also live right in their presence so it would be easy for them to honor and obey me. The way I live right, in their presence, is by imitating the characteristics of GOD. That's why Paul told us in chapter 4, everything light produces is good. The danger of me walking in the flesh before my children is, they end up picking up my fleshly characteristics. If my children become aware of what's right and what's wrong, I can't get upset with them if they choose not to respect me because I choose to walk in my flesh.

For example, remember Paul told us in Ephesians chapter 5 the desires of the flesh are sexual sin, perversion of any kind, greed, filthiness, perversion, will cause us not to inherit the kingdom of GOD. I can't get upset with my children if they choose not to respect me because I choose to practice these sins. Especially if they know that it is wrong. Paul said in chapter 5 verse 3, This is not appropriate behavior for GOD's holy people. Even if I choose to live inappropriately in front of my children, they are still responsible to obey and honor me as their parent. Why? Paul says in verse 1, for this is right.

Now, it is not right for them to mimic my inappropriate behavior because this obey means to obey in the Lord. But it is right for them to honor and obey me as their parent. So, if provoking them causes them not to honor and obey me, their days are cut short. Then, it's almost as if I'm somewhat the cause. Even though they are the ones that's responsible for their days being long upon the land.

Could you imagine what the reward would be for a child who still chose to respect their parents even when their parents chose to live inappropriately and provoked them to anger? But, could you also imagine the punishment to a parent that chose to live inappropriately and cause their children to disobey and not honor them as their parents because their parents provoked them to anger? So, basically, what's the message? Live according to the SPIRIT so our behavior doesn't cause our children to dishonor us, which would cause them not to obey us. I guess Paul was right when he said everything the SPIRIT produces is good. Now we have a clearer understanding of everything our flesh produces is darkness.

Let's put this into context. The balance of kids obeying and honoring their parents and parents not provoking their children brings unity to the Body of CHRIST. Paul told us in chapter 5, I speak concerning CHRIST and The Church. Once again, Paul is not pausing from his message about unity in The Body of CHRIST to deal with parents and their children. For there to be unity in the Body of CHRIST, there has to be unity amongst the believers. There has to be unity between husbands and wives and between parents and children.

Advice to Slaves & Masters
Verses 5-9

Now, let's deal with, what I think to be, one of the most controversial passages in Scripture, which is found in verse 5. Slaves, obey your earthly masters with proper respect. Be as sincere as you are when you obey CHRIST. A lot of people don't like this particular passage. They feel that it was put in the Bible to make us a good slave. But, guess what took place when Paul wrote this letter? Slavery. Like I said before, Paul wasn't speaking to society, he was speaking to The Body of CHRIST.

That meant there were some who were in slavery that accepted CHRIST as their Savior. Not only were there slaves that accepted CHRIST, but there were also slave owners that accepted CHRIST. Now, in society, the relationship between slave owners and slaves was one of authority. However, once a slave and a slave master became saved, they no longer had a relationship of authority. They are now a part of The Body of CHRIST. They are now considered brothers and sisters in CHRIST.

When you look at Paul's message to the slave and slave owner, it was almost as if the slave got saved and the slave owner wasn't. Or if the slave owner became saved, and the slave wasn't. Verses 6-9 says, Don't obey them only while you're being watched, as if you merely wanted to please people. But obey like slaves who belong to CHRIST, who have a deep desire to do what GOD wants them to do. Serve eagerly as if you were serving your heavenly master and not merely serving human masters. You know that your heavenly master will reward all of us for whatever good we do, whether we're slaves or free people. Masters, treat your slaves with respect. Don't threaten a slave. You know that there is one master in heaven who has authority over both of you, and HE doesn't play favorites.

Once a slave became saved, there was a certain mindset the slave was supposed to have towards the slave owner. Once the slave owner became saved, there was a certain mindset he was supposed to have towards the slave. As far as the slave is concerned, Galatians teaches us, as believers, that even though you can be oppressed by society, you can still have freedom in CHRIST. If a slave becomes saved, and the slave owner is not, then the slave owner is still going to look at the slave as a slave even though the slave is now saved. If the slave, who is now saved, is following the teachings of Paul, it just may cause the slave owner to accept CHRIST for himself. The same way a saved slave is supposed to treat his unsaved slave owner, the slave owner is supposed to treat his unsaved slave with respect. Because hopefully, the slave would choose to accept CHRIST for themselves.

Like I mentioned earlier, a saved slave owner can't be a follower of CHRIST who gives us freedom, and keep another believer in bondage. What did Paul tell us in Ephesians chapter 4 verses 4-6? There is One Body and One Spirit, just as you were called in one hope of your calling; one Lord, one Faith, one baptism; one GOD and Father of all, who is above all, and through all, and in you all. If we are part of the same One Body that's controlled by the same One SPIRIT, and the same GOD is Father of us all, how can someone keep you in bondage if we are a part of the same One Faith? They won't.

During slavery in the United States, yes, they manipulated the Scriptures to keep us in bondage. They used it out of evil and deceit. Slave owners did not respect their slaves, they just wanted their slaves to be obedient servants. How the slaves' owners manipulated the Scriptures back then, if I was a slave, I wouldn't want anything to do with their religion. They manipulated the Scriptures to keep themselves in superiority. Paul wrote the Scriptures to keep us in unity. You can't have unity in The Body if there is superiority.

Paul says in Galatians 3:26-29, For you are all sons of GOD through Faith in CHRIST JESUS. For as many of you as were baptized into CHRIST have put on CHRIST. There is neither Jew nor Greek, there is neither slave nor free, there is neither male nor female; for you are all one in CHRIST JESUS. And if you are CHRIST's, then you are Abraham's seed, and heirs according to the promise.

Put On All the Armor That GOD Supplies
Verses 10-20

When Paul wrote this letter to the Christians in Ephesus, Paul was talking to The Body of CHRIST. The believers that had confessed JESUS as Lord and not to society. Let's continue to keep everything in context. Paul's teaching regarding spiritual warfare is going to be helpful to every believer. Unity is the key. If The Body of CHRIST is divided, then how are we going to fight spiritual warfare as a Body?

One thing we should have learned by now is, that we can't fight spiritual warfare separated. GOD never gave all the power to one believer. The only person that walked around with all power was CHRIST. When CHRIST left, CHRIST said himself, greater work than these shall you do. (John 14:12) However, not as individuals, as The Body of CHRIST. We represent The Body of CHRIST.

As the Body of CHRIST, it's our job to express the desires of CHRIST. The Bible says let this mind be in you that was also in CHRIST JESUS. (Philippians 2:5) If we are The Body of CHRIST, then The Body is supposed to execute the commands of the Head. The sad reality is, we have allowed the enemy to separate The Body, whereby we are no longer performing the desires of the Head. The enemy knows when we are on one accord as One Body and One Spirit, one hope; one Lord, one Faith, one baptism; one GOD and Father, then The Body is effective when it's time to battle spiritual wickedness.

In the closing of his letter, Paul gives a list of instructions regarding spiritual warfare. The Church is supposed to be spiritually equipped to fight spiritual warfare. Chapter 3:10, Paul said GOD equipped The Church so that through the church, he could let the rulers and authorities in heaven know HIS infinite wisdom. Not only are we supposed to have the power to speak to nations as a Church Body. But, we're supposed to have the authority to speak to spiritual wickedness and principalities in high places.

Spiritual wickedness in high places is not afraid of The Church. Why? The Church doesn't know how to come together and allow GOD's power to work through us as a Body. We are more concerned about getting emotionally aroused than we are about tapping into the power that can bring down strongholds. It's very important for us to have unity in The Body. When there's unity, in The Body, then The Body can effectively let the rulers and authorities in heaven know HIS infinite wisdom. The devil knows, if he can separate The Church Body, then The Body has no power or authority. When The Church has no unity, The Church can't fight spiritual wickedness in high places because we're too busy fighting each other in the flesh. I may sound repetitive but this is a must for The Body of Christ.

Let's take a look at what Paul tells us in verses 10 - 12 Finally, my brethren, be strong in the Lord and in the power of HIS might. Put on the whole armor of GOD, that you may be able to stand against the wiles of the devil. For we do not wrestle against flesh and blood, but against principalities, against powers, against the rulers of the darkness of this age, against spiritual hosts of wickedness in the heavenly places.

When we are fighting each other in the flesh, what we're not realizing is, we are really wrestling against spiritual wickedness that's causing us to fight each other in the flesh. While we are fighting each other in the flesh, no one is revealing GOD's infinite wisdom to spiritual wickedness. Verse 12 says For we do not wrestle against flesh and blood. Who are we wrestling with? Against the rulers of the darkness. My question to The Church is, why are we wrestling and fighting with one another when we're supposed to be revealing? You can't fight spiritual wickedness in the flesh. You can only fight spiritual wickedness in high places in the Spirit.

How do we fight spiritual wickedness in the Spirit? I'm glad you asked. Look at verse 13, Therefore, take up the whole armor of GOD, that you may be able to withstand in the evil day, and having done all, to stand. The only way for me to be able to speak GOD's infinite wisdom to spiritual wickedness in high places is not by fighting or wrestling, but by taking up the whole armor of GOD. GOD does not give us HIS armor to fight, HE gives us HIS armor to stand.

When The Church does stand, we can stand and speak HIS wisdom with authority. We can stand and speak HIS wisdom with power. So, now the question is if we're supposed to be dealing with spiritual wickedness in high places by revealing GOD's infinite wisdom, why are we wrestling spiritual wickedness in the flesh?

Verse 12 told us we were not wrestling one another in the flesh. Our problem is, spiritual wickedness is causing us to fight each other in the flesh, which is causing us to be ineffective in the Spirit. The reason The Church Body is not being effective is the Spirit and the government can stop The Church from coming together, is all because spiritual wickedness is causing us to fight each other in the flesh.

I know a lot of people are saying the church is still The Church, even if we don't come together. My question is, how is The Church being effective by us being divided? Trust me, I understand that the building does not represent The Church. But division doesn't represent The Church either. Acts 2:1 says, When Pentecost, the fiftieth day after Passover, came, all the believers were together in one place. Verse 4 comes in and says, after they came together in one place on one accord, then, all the believers were filled with the HOLY SPIRIT. Then all the believers were filled with power. Then all the believers were able to reveal the wisdom of GOD. Then all the believers were able to speak in the language of those that were present. Watch this, they were able to reveal GOD's wisdom to those that needed to hear it.

In the next few verses, after Paul tells us to take up the whole armor of GOD. He uses armor in the natural to represent the benefits in the Spirit. We shouldn't focus on the armor in the natural, but how it would benefit us in the Spirit. Look at what Paul says in verses 14 – 18, Stand therefore... Stand for what Paul? That you can be able, not to fight but be able to stand... having girded your waist with truth, having put on the breastplate of righteousness, and having shod your feet with the preparation of the gospel of peace; above all, taking the shield of Faith with which you will be able to quench all the fiery darts of the wicked one. And take the helmet of salvation, and the sword of the Spirit, which is the word of GOD; praying always with all prayer and supplication in the Spirit, being watchful to this end with all perseverance and supplication for all the saints—.

Paul didn't describe the different pieces of armor for us to focus on the natural. He gave it to us so we can see the benefits they have in the Spirit. When you take away the natural pieces of armor, look at what you are left with; truth, righteousness, the gospel of peace, faith, salvation, the Word of GOD, and praying in the Spirit. All of these things help me to stand against spiritual wickedness so I'm able to reveal GOD's wisdom to the rulers of darkness.

To back up everything that Paul has just taught us about having the authority to stand and reveal GOD's wisdom, look at what Paul says in verses 19 and 20, and for me, that utterance may be given to me, that I may open my mouth boldly to make known the mystery of the gospel, for which I am an ambassador in chains; that in it I may speak boldly, as I ought to speak. GOD has equipped The Church to stand and speak boldly. It's until The Church can come together on one accord, that we'll be able to stand and speak the infinite wisdom of GOD boldly, regardless of the circumstance.

In verse 20, Paul says my circumstance is, I am in prison. But even my circumstances can't control my authority to speak boldly. Until The Church realizes that we are more effective when we come together on one accord; then The Church will be able to speak the infinite wisdom of GOD boldly and make things happen. If GOD has given us as a Body with this type of authority over darkness, then we also have authority over sickness. All we have to do, as a Body, is boldly make known GOD's infinite wisdom to sickness. Just like GOD has given us the authority to speak boldly to spiritual wickedness. HE has also given us the authority to speak boldly to sickness.

We should be making it known to sickness that GOD is a Healer. We should be making it known that GOD is a Deliverer. The reason The Church can't make the infinite wisdom of GOD known and the government can tell The Church what to do instead of The Church making known the infinite wisdom of GOD is because The Church is separated and divided and not on one accord.

The sad reality is, The Church is the only one that can make known GOD's infinite wisdom to spiritual wickedness in high places. That is why Paul tells the believers in verse 20 to pray for him that he might be able to speak boldly as he ought to. As believers, we are commissioned by GOD to speak boldly to spiritual wickedness in high places.

Greetings From Paul
Verses 21-24

As Paul gets ready to close out his message to the believers in the city of Ephesus, Paul says in verses 21-24, I'm sending Tychicus to you. He is our dear brother and a faithful deacon in the Lord's work. He will tell you everything that is happening to me so that you will know how I'm getting along. That's why I'm sending him to you so that you may know how we're doing and that he may encourage you. May God the Father and the Lord Jesus Christ give our brothers and sisters peace and love along with Faith. HIS favor is with everyone who has an undying love for our Lord Jesus Christ.

Tychius was a companion to Paul who often traveled with Paul. Paul had given him the responsibility as a messenger to the various churches. As Paul is describing Tychius to the believers, it was almost as if Paul was describing him, not only for them to feel comfortable about his mission, but as an example for every thing Paul has been teaching them in his letter.

- Tychius was a beloved brother, check!
- He was a man who believed in JESUS and demonstrated it by loving others, check!
- He treated other believers as brothers and sisters in CHRIST, check!
- He was Faithful by doing his part in The Body, check!
- He stuck to his assignment, check!
- He was obedient, check!

As we come together, let us be mindful of the importance of us coming together in unity. Spiritual wickedness already knows, 'Together we will stand, but divided we shall fall.' Let us stand in the authority that GOD has given to us as a Body and let's let the rulers and authorities in heaven know GOD's infinite wisdom.

Notes

Nasa.gov. (Apr 14, 2020). 50 Years Ago: "Houston, We've Had a Problem" Retrieved from
https://www.nasa.gov/feature/50-years-ago-houston-we-ve-had-a-problem

Stedman, R. C. (2012). Adventuring through the Bible: A comprehensive guide to the entire Bible.
Discovery House Publishers.

CPSIA information can be obtained
at www.ICGtesting.com
Printed in the USA
BVHW041035081121
621073BV00016B/922